James Hedderwick

Lays of Middle Age

And Other Poems

James Hedderwick

Lays of Middle Age
And Other Poems

ISBN/EAN: 9783337006587

Printed in Europe, USA, Canada, Australia, Japan

Cover: Foto ©Thomas Meinert / pixelio.de

More available books at **www.hansebooks.com**

Lays

of

Middle Age:

and

Other Poems.

By *James Hedderwick*, LL.D.

WILLIAM BLACKWOOD & SONS,
EDINBURGH AND LONDON.
1889.

THE Volume, entitled 'LAYS OF MIDDLE AGE, and OTHER POEMS,' was originally published by Messrs. Macmillan & Co. as far back as 1859. It has long been out of print, and the Author has found occupation for the leisure of his more advanced years in preparing the present Pocket Edition for the press.

While the 'Lays' are largely made up of reflections appropriate to 'Middle Age,' they were mainly suggested by incidents or events—personal or public—either occurring when they were written, or remembered from a prior date. The several interesting decades which have since elapsed have been quite as fruitful of themes inviting poetical treatment, but no attempt has been made to encumber the poem, viewed in its homogeneous character, with additions in which the standpoint would necessarily have been different. Accordingly, the first and leading section of this little Book is simply a reprint of the work of thirty years ago, with a few trifling emendations.

As regards the 'Other Poems,' a good many alterations have been made. Some have been altogether omitted, and their places supplied by a select number written at various times, although, with one exception, previously printed elsewhere. The portion of the Volume thus re-edited has also been differently arranged and grouped; while the Pieces which are new to this edition are, for the guidance of the reader, marked with an asterisk.

It may be observed that the work and worry of Journalism, in the midst of which most of the following pages were composed, are unfavourable to any considerable achievement in the field of polite letters. Of this the Author is abundantly, if not painfully conscious. But however far he may have fallen short of his own poetic desires and ideals, there are, he may be pardoned for stating, some things included in this re-issue which have won commendation in very gratifying quarters; and he, therefore, ventures to express a hope that, in the form in which they are now presented, they may meet with an equally sympathetic and perhaps wider welcome.

The few pictorial embellishments with which the letter-press is interspersed are from the pencil of a young Scottish artist, Mr. David Gauld.

ROCKBANK HOUSE,
 HELENSBURGH, N.B.

Contents.

LAYS OF MIDDLE AGE.

	PAGE		PAGE
Reconciled,	1	Too Much we Marvel,	43
The Release,	3	Sunshine and Storm,	45
Thought Pictures,	4	A Brighter Clime,	46
Nature Inexhaustible,	6	Severed,	48
Books,	7	From My Window,	49
A Dark Background,	9	Helpless,	51
Up the Stream,	10	Rich Only,	52
The Inner Life,	12	Whom have I Known?	54
A Miser's Treasure,	13	Heart-Ache,	55
Cheerfulness in Age,	15	Epithalamium,	57
The New Cemetery,	16	In the Street,	58
Once and Again,	18	The Revolt,	60
Hereditary Monarchy,	19	Victory,	61
Passed Away,	21	When?	63
Confidential,	22	The Resumption,	64
In Vain,	24	Where are the Friends?	66
Alone,	25	The Inevitable,	67
Genius and Presumption,	27	Too Eager,	69
Posthumous,	28	Sabbath in the Country,	70
The Crown of Song,	30	The Grave,	72
War,	31	A Contrast,	73
After the Fight,	33	The Eclipse,	75
Consolation,	34	Poetic Melancholy,	76
The Majority,	36	Under the Waves,	78
Changed Scenes,	37	The New-Year,	79
Aspiration,	39	When I Reflect,	81
Fame,	40	Middle Age,	82
Unwritten Fancies,	42		

MISCELLANEOUS.

	PAGE		PAGE
Waiting for the Ship,	87	*In the Night,*	102
Sorrow and Song,	90	*To a Cowslip,*	105
The Twin Sisters,	92	*The Emigrants,*	107
The Sky-Lark,	95	*Shakespeare,*	109
By the Sea-Side,	98	*Household Words,*	113
The Stars,	100	*Any Man of Himself,*	117

ELEGIAC.

	PAGE		PAGE
First Grief,	123	*Flo's Photo,*	134
Home Trial,	127	*Storm and Calm,*	142

TWO ODES.

	PAGE
Victoria,	149
A Midsummer Day's Dream,	157

Lays of Middle Age:

and

Other Poems.

LAYS OF MIDDLE AGE.

I.—RECONCILED.

Our loved one lay in depth of suffering,
And there was suffering in all the rooms,
Wide-eyed suspense amid the sickly glooms,
And faltering prayers which no relief could bring.
We saw the agony we could not ease,
As of one drowning in the sight of shore.
At length came lessening pain with more disease—
Came the calm end—a calm unknown before—
A calm rebuke to mortal sorrowing.

Even as in tears we gazed, the silent balm
Fell sweet within, for we began to see
A preparation in the agony,
Until we knew to uplift the grateful psalm,
Reading GOD's mercy in the tortured breast,
And thinking all was right when all was still.
How could we part with him we loved the best?
But came the calm upon the mighty ill,
And we were sadly calm to see him calm.

Thoughts of that hour have tuned my soul to know
The beauty palaced in the face of Death.
How easeful is the absence of all breath!
How soothed the pulse whose tides have ceased to flow!
Who brands with 'tyrant' him who bears release
Up to the martyr's stake, and isles the deep
Through all its raging waste with shores of peace?
O angel Death! that bringest healing sleep
To bosoms wounded with a hopeless woe!

II.—THE RELEASE.

LIKE a world-weary student, free to rove
For ease and health by fair poetic streams,
To cull the flowers that only grow in dreams,
For simple tastes to censure or approve,
Would I with grateful heart make sorrow sweet.
The fitful blooms which now in pride I twine
For thee, dear Friend! may wither at thy feet:
Yet haply may'st thou, in their transient shine,
See gleams of beauty through thine eyes of love.

No coming darkness striketh needless fears:
Yet, looking onward o'er life's glittering meads,
I spy a road and wonder where it leads.
A chill is wafted from the fleeting years.
Great Heaven! what doom it were to walk alone
To the final Mystery! but hand in hand,
With all the generation journeying on,
We face with courage due the shadowy land,
And scarce would lag behind our marching peers.

And so, best loved! each sad and gradual trace
Our future may reveal of springtime past
Will catch a soothing from the splendour cast
On Autumn woods. Though each with each keep pace,
And age but mark our long companionship,
If mellowing love of mine new joy illume
Within thy soul, and crown with smiles thy lip,
To my unstraying eyes through life shall bloom
A youth of beauty in thy matron face.

III.—THOUGHT PICTURES.

*N*OON walks the earth in Summer's sultry pride.
Bewilder'd butterflies of many hues
Flatter the flowers to yield their honey-dews:
Where the leaves tremble and the shadows hide
Are voices wrestling for the mastery
Of fluted melody in feather'd throats:
White sails are gleaming on the quiet sea:
Along the craggy shore the white gull floats:
For clinging odours scarce a breeze can glide.

Lays of Middle Age.

The tawny herd-boy wields his wand of power
O'er nibbled mountain steeps; nor knows nor thinks
How bless'd his station, nor what golden links
Of memory he forgeth hour by hour:
The fragrant kine lie languid in the heat:
Half hid in leaves and smoke the village dreams:
The river glideth at the angler's feet:
Child-voices cheer the glade where beauty gleams
In many a sunny glint and simple flower.

Meet scenes to environ a poetic home!
Ye, from lone impulse of the beautiful,
I joy to paint, even under skies made dull
By hovering smoke, amid a dreary boom
Of city traffic sounding evermore,
Happy to feel that round about me lies
A world as fresh and splendid as of yore,
Whence come sweet airs like breaths from Paradise,
And thoughts like sunbeams gladdening as they come!

IV.—NATURE INEXHAUSTIBLE.

'Wiled by the charm that lies in measured tones,
I grow enamour'd of a patient tune;
Yet lives there now a beauty in the moon,
Or any music in the night wind's moans,
That has not wrought enchantment many a year?
Seen was the universe with clearer eye,
And heard its melodies with finer ear,
By generations in the dust that lie,
And lo, their laureates on immortal thrones!'

Thus mused I wandering in the year's sweet prime,
At feud with slavery of commonplace—
Seeking how I my casual lay might grace
With thoughts new-borrow'd from the budding-time.
The poet's richest harvest is the Spring.
Yet every opening flower I spied was wreathed
With some old bard's most gentle fancying,
Like the soft incense which itself outbreathed.
Oh, wherefore load it with superfluous rhyme?

Lays of Middle Age.

Athwart my dawn of hopes there crept a chill,
Like morning frost among the youngling buds;
But when I look'd upon the lands and floods,
And the clear azure, arch'd from hill to hill,
To win new larks to heaven—that hour there came,
Like a rich bride to her adorer's arms,
A summer feeling, like a glow of shame,
To think how I had wrong'd great Nature's charms,
Renew'd and beauteous for the poet still.

V.—BOOKS.

As mong the wondrous growths of some hot clime
The traveller pauses, wilder'd with excess
Of trackless herbage, plants of gaudy dress,
And stately palms—so I, through prose and rhyme,
Thick as the forest with its drowsy plumes,
In vain essay to compass in a life
The magic splendours and immortal blooms
Scattered o'er pages as the foliage rife
Of smothering summers faint with musk and thyme.

What need of more? In the celestial bowers
Must new stars blossom? Must the burden'd shore
Of the world's continents hunger for more
Far-stretching wealth of shells? Must vernal hours
Alive with birds for richer music pine?
Wherefore more books? Why dip another pen
In the ink that burns by alchemy divine
Like DANAE's fount, when our tired age of men
Is drench'd and flooded with its aureate showers?

Ah me! we wander in a tangled maze.
There is no waste. So, let the eternal gold
From genius' mint be scatter'd myriadfold:
Never a star was launch'd but its fine rays
Took some small shade of darkness from the night;
The stream that sings unseen among the ferns
Bears welcome increase to the ocean's might;
Even the minutest flower the sense discerns
Enriches all the breaths of summer days.

VI.—A DARK BACKGROUND.

ONE said to me, with the meek plea in his face
Of failing health, 'I have a picture, sir,
I wish you much to see.' At secret stir
Of sympathy, I sought his dwelling-place
Where poverty sat bare. From childhood's eyes
Yearn'd looks of age and urged him to fresh toil.
The canvas show'd 'A Dream of Paradise,'
Fairly conceived, and colour'd well in oil,
With EVE's young blush, and ADAM's lofty grace.

It was the only sunshine in the room,
For all the rays of gladness from around
Were gather'd in itself. The garden-ground
Dewy and prank'd with flowers of wondrous bloom,
The skies cerulean, and the first fine forms
Of all humanity, shone like a gleam
Of peaceful azure 'mid a rack of storms.
Much talk'd he of the beauty of his dream—
Much saw I of the sadness of his doom.

Some faults the picture had; but when he roll'd
A paper forth and read—'A poor attempt,
From every sin of genius quite exempt;'
And added, 'It of course came back unsold,'
I had no eyes but for its loveliness,
No feeling but of sorrow for the tear
That came in witness of his dumb distress.
Ah me! that Paradise so sweet and clear!
The sickly artist and the children old!

VII.—UP THE STREAM.

MUSING on aged faces, oft I read
Their history backward. Woman! whom I see
Like dry fruit wrinkled, I can trace in thee
The maiden beauty that was thine indeed;
Smooth thy scored forehead, and about it braid
Soft girlish tresses; open wide thine eyes;
Round out thy cheeks for artless blushes made;
Ruby thy lips to smile at flatteries;
And row thy mouth with pearls of native breed.

Thou walk'st as under burdens.   Who so light
In the old century, when thy nimble feet
Leapt to untiring violins in the fleet
And boisterous country-dance?   Oh age's spite!
Dost frown upon the joys 'twas thine to share?
Thou art grave now; yet, at Medean touch
Of fancy, I can see thee young and fair,
In jewell'd splendour, mocking age's crutch,
And whirling in the mazes of the night.

What rivals once had barter'd half their gains
And all their sleep for thy conceded kiss!
Do these old lips their low-breathed ardours miss,
And fondly mumble still of love and chains?
I plump them back to rosebud poutings, bland
And beautiful in maidhood, and I own
The charms that put a price upon the hand
Thou gav'st, in pity of his constant moan,
To him, now old, who laughs at love-sick swains!

VIII.—THE INNER LIFE.

FROM tender thinkings to the eye's fine lid
A dew comes sweetly. Unforgotten sights,
Escapes of travel, chance-spent glorious nights
With those whose memory like a pyramid
Is broadly based and higher than all mists,
Our daily lot of fortune or of wrong,
We tell in fearless prose though the world lists.
But all have secrets which, like griefs in song,
Disguised are utter'd or kept always hid.

Some early cross or long-repented sin
Cowers in the heart, of daylight eyes afraid;
Some life-aim miss'd, or failure bitter made
By jeering tongues; some grovelling shame of kin
Draining mute drops; some haunting form and face
More precious than the spoils of many books:—
All these we lock as in a secret place
The letters of dead loves, for aching looks
When clouds of loneliness make gloom within.

But even the silent treasury of the breast,
By pride lone-sentinell'd, has a secret spring
Which lays it open. Music's sorrowing,
Through echo of some voice long years at rest,
May touch it groping in the tearful dark.
Some tale which has a mystery of truth
May on a sudden hit the invisible mark,
And charm the cloister'd memories of youth
To tears which but to weep is to be blest.

IX.—A MISER'S TREASURE.

*I*N a small chamber, cobwebb'd 'gainst the sky,
Where the celestial lights forgotten were,
Sat one of juiceless veins, a usurer,
Gloating on gold with hungry hand and eye.
For him the world had naught of beauty save
The yellow shimmer of his counted heaps,
Nor music but the chink his guineas gave :
These drank he madly in his tortured sleeps,
And ever as he drank his life ran dry.

For him the seasons pattern'd all in vain
The joyous fields.   In vain for him the streams
Made breezy melody.   No voice of dreams
Came to him from the sea.   The russet wain,
Ringing through woodland lanes, was naught to him.
For him the grove was tuneless, and the skies,
Bounteous in showers, were vile.   His vision dim
Saw not the flowers laugh up with liquid eyes
At balmy whisper of the summer rain.

His neighbours wonder'd who might be his heir,
They call'd him 'miser,' 'wretch,' 'poor grubbing worm,'
'His mind,' said one, 'is crookëd as his form,
And more of earth.'   Another envying sware,
'By Heaven! his very face—his every look
Is stamp'd with greed.'   To gibes he was a stone:
But from a secret drawer he sometimes took,
For tearful gaze when he was quite alone,
A faded writing and a lock of hair!

X.—CHEERFULNESS IN AGE.

I PASS'D a pleasant evening with LEIGH HUNT.
The room was squared with books, 'mong which I spied
Rows of the Tuscan poets.   On each side
The fire we sat ;—he, as appear'd his wont,
Sipping refreshful draughts of sober tea.
Wiry and thin, a figure tall he show'd,
Unbent with years.   His gray hair lankily
Over his ears hung straight.   His dark eyes glow'd.
He wore the conscious poet in his front.

He talk'd with store of happy similes
Of his own toils ; of trials all but past ;
Of honours coming to his age at last ;
Of stubborn heights surmounted by degrees ;
Of KEATS, love-sicken'd with the beautiful ;
Of all poetic sweets on Hybla hived ;
Of him whose conquering eye was crown and rule—
KEAN—how immortal could his art have lived !
To listen well was all my art to please.

Some men there are of prompt achieving mind
Who wait not any gale to waft them on,
But move like ships that walk the seas alone,
And take its ancient uses from the wind:
He, the fine bard of tragic Rimini,
Seem'd one of these on that delicious night.
I mark'd his soul of native buoyancy,
And I was cheer'd from sitting in the light
Of his white hairs, and wish'd me of his kind.

XI.—THE NEW CEMETERY.

As any lawn this burial-place is even.
Save the white head-stones with their dates of woe,
It yields no sign of those who rest below.
To mourning eyes no outward mark is given
That the smooth sward holds all the heart regrets.
The graves are level as the empty beds
That stand at home with unstirr'd coverlets;
Or as the prairie-turf the traveller treads
Where never spade has delved or ploughshare driven.

Lays of Middle Age.

Our simple fathers in their church-yards old
O'er the loved dead heap'd up the grassy mound,
As they would shape the sleeper underground
For friends in dewy twilight to behold.
O fitting couch for grief to lean upon!
It caught an earlier greeting from the day,
A later blessing from the setting sun.
Earth's kindly sob it seem'd o'er kindred clay.
The heaving turf lay lightly on the mould.

But here the callous grass shows no more sorrow
Than o'er the drown'd the placid ocean-plain.
It swells not up to meet the eyes' sweet rain.
What footing may the mounting spirit borrow
From this roll'd flat? The dead are blotted out—
Buried, and earth no richer—vague their sleep!
We try to trace our own, almost in doubt
If they are there. To-day we idly weep,
Or faintly murmur of a golden morrow.

XII.—ONCE AND AGAIN.

ONCE as I stray'd a student, happiest then,
What time the Summer's garniture was on,
Beneath the princely shades of Kensington,
A girl I spied whose years might number ten,
With full round eyes, and fair soft English face.
A liveried lackey upon either side
Her palfrey walk'd afoot. With equal pace
Follow'd a mounted dame at distance wide.
They thrid the turfy paths scarce seen of men.

From the surroundings of the maiden-child
I guess'd her Royal state and destiny.
Across the gulf which lay 'twixt her and me,
In those green alleys where the seasons smiled
Alike on both, though fortune most on her,
I dared to look, for she came slowly near.
Features like hers were radiant otherwhere.
Save for her high-bred pallor, calm and clear,
She might have bloom'd a flower on any wild.

Again I saw her. Alter'd was her mien.
A matron flush upon her aspect show'd
The high sun flaming on her noonday road.
One call'd her wife—some mother—millions queen!
No more to her the small birds only sang.
The fluttering streets, as she went floating past,
Were bank'd with people whose hoarse voices rang
With loud 'VICTORIAS!' Ah the difference vast!—
The flaring city and those alleys green.

XIII.—HEREDITARY MONARCHY.

'WHEREFORE,' a vain boy ask'd, 'should England
A crown hereditary, to be conferr'd   [own
Perchance on feeble brows?' A sage who heard
Thus answer'd—'Argued well: the great alone
Should hold great sway: our king of men should rule.
But which were king should twenty kings arise?
To know its greatest men the world is dull,
And to the loudest yields the largest prize.
Whom, with thy choice, would'st thou this hour enthrone?'

The unripe youth exclaim'd—'Can our brave land
Be barren ever of heroic men?
Live they not now, with sword, or tongue, or pen,
To prove their mighty title to command?'
'They live,' replied the sage, 'and in such force,
That each, in virtue of his kingly mood,
Heading a party fierce with faction's curse,
Might covet triumph through his country's blood,
Till order came but from a tyrant's hand.'

A mild and temper'd rule is England's dower,
Won from a wise and stubborn ancestry.
What safety for her charter of the free
In strong hands trembling with precarious power?
Our old inheritance be still our pride.
Happy the land where each may rise and shine,
From turmoil safe, uncaring to decide
Which in the forest is the tallest pine,
Which in[1] the garden is the fairest flower.

XIV.—PASSED AWAY.

PEACE dwells at last with poor ELIZABETH,
Wife of my trusted friend. The end has come.
There is no tremulous voice to call him home;
And yet he goes, and sits alone with Death,
Though useless now his tender ministries.
There is no fretting at his absence now:
Yet sits he by her side, and sadly tries
To gather soothing from her tranquil brow
And stony bosom without pulse or breath.

The fever'd watching has been all in vain;
The struggle now has ended in defeat:
Yet in her aspect is a rest so sweet
That were she waked she might again complain.
Oh who could wish to wring her human heart
With one pang more? But past is every fear:
Still'd by the mystery that would not start
Although a cannon thunder'd at her ear—
Although her little infant cried with pain.

Ah me! that one so beautiful should die!
Full on her widow'd husband ere she went,
Like light within a shatter'd tenement,
Linger'd the last love-lustre of her eye.
On the vague threshold of the unseen life
She paused; then feebly from her finger took
The golden circlet of the mortal wife,
Placed it on his, with reassuring look,
And wedded him to immortality.

XV.—CONFIDENTIAL.

HIGH rose the noon. I had an hour to spare
In REGINALD'S garden, trimm'd with matchless grace.
Warbled that day a spirit in the place,
Like music knowing that the flowers were fair;
And I was happy, but my friend was sad.
So spake I rallying—'Thou art out of tune
With this sweet Eden and its voices glad!
What wintry cloud should dim his sky of June,
Of health and fortune who has ample share?'

Sighing, he said—'A truth which many prove,
With me, too slowly fear'd, has come to pass.
As perilous for foot as adder's grass
Are all the flowery ways of youthful love.'
'Sad fate,' said I, 'to love in spite of scorn!'
'Thou judgest wrong,' cried doleful REGINALD:
'Some leagues away a maiden pines forlorn;
Thither to soothe her I am hourly call'd;
Honour cries 'On!' and yet I fail to move!'

More question'd I. At length he thus explain'd:—
'I have a cousin whom I once adored.
Ere yet I left my teens I long implored,
Until her girlish troth at last I gain'd
By oaths which time has turn'd to perjuries!
Her beauty now is wither'd to my view,
But still her heart is faithful to my lies!
As I wax false she weareth doubly true:
Her love is torture now that mine has waned!'

XVI.—IN VAIN.

'PITY,' I said—as on a rustic form
We sat us down, myself and REGINALD,
Where happy birds their true loves madrigall'd—
'Pity that in this nook, where frost and storm
Would seem unknown, the imps of ill should lurk,
Like fairy cankers in the velvet buds;
Pity that alien thoughts should inly work,
And gnaw with grief a maiden's blushful moods,
As berries oft are hollow'd by a worm.

'Helpless as clinging fruit upon the tree
She hung upon thy love. Say she has lost
Some outward bloom, through hopes delay'd and cross'd,
Hath it not gone to enrich her trust in thee
Beyond thy frail desert to parallel?
If haply some new beauty thou should'st wed,
That beauty faded, where will be its spell?
By oldest memory is love best fed,
As farthest founts swell largest to the sea.

'Why should thy true love any longer seek
To wear the bashful beauty on her brow
Once woo'd and worshipp'd? Where thy whisper'd vow?
Flowers come when airs invite. Beauty as weak
As flowers or tears, the flattery should sip
That it is still the bribe of constant love.
Cheated of that it dies.' Upon his lip
A passion trembled and with judgment strove;—
But left the lilies in the maiden's cheek!

XVII.—ALONE.

So REGINALD is still a bachelor—
Not young, yet youthful—studious of his ease—
His only thought how best himself to please.
Of richest wines he has an endless store.
These are his pride, and oft as lovingly
As they were children he will tell their age.
His city house, his mansion by the sea,
Alternately his jovial hours engage.
So great his wealth it hourly groweth more.

A little luck, a little keen address,
A little kindly help in time of need,
A little industry and touch of greed,
Have made his life a singular success;
And he asks homage for his splendid gains,
Paying the flattery in meats and drinks!
Applauding friends he daily entertains,
To ease him of himself. Sometimes he thinks
If he were poor his friends might love him less.

Gray-headed REGINALD! he has royal parts,
And in all circles fills an honour'd seat.
Yet vain for him are maiden's accents sweet:
At wedded slavery and henpeck'd hearts
He jeers and laughs; though, when the nights are cold,
The tables empty, and he feels alone,
A memory breaks of purer joys of old;
And, selfish to the last, he thinks of one
Who might have soothed him with her gentle arts!

XVIII.—GENIUS AND PRESUMPTION.

A NOISE of talk was in the public ways.
One had arrived the city's votes to claim,
At whose approach the invisible trump of Fame
Blew into life the echoes of all praise.
His song had stirr'd the dust of buried Rome;
His pen in England's annals had struck life;
His voice had made a muttering Senate dumb.
Lo! a throng'd hall, with expectation rife,
And ears attent, and eyes of eager gaze!

MACAULAY rose;—a man of sturdy build,
With ageing hair, and face of dusky hue
Lit up with restless eyes of luminous blue;
His frame erect as with disdain to yield
To the high task to which it was upnerved.
In the first lull of welcome and applause,
His voice bespoke a soul that never swerved
In its devotion to a chosen cause,
And all the admiring multitude was thrill'd.

His arguments like deftly-wielded swords
Flash'd and struck home.   When he resumed his seat,
A demagogue rose grimly to his feet,
And flung his pittance 'gainst the master's hoards
Of thought and knowledge;—clamour'd down, yet cool,
He talk'd in tones of ignorant dispute!
Oh much I marvell'd at the matchless fool!—
I so content to listen humbly mute,
And gather wisdom from the great man's words.

XIX.—POSTHUMOUS.

She sat where sorrow is content to dwell;
From pious words she drew unwonted calm;
Her voice was lowly in the shouted psalm,
As the low murmur of an empty shell
That to one ear alone breathes out its sighs;
In crape and cambric she was chastely clad,
But most she wore her mourning in her eyes:
Close by her side a lovely boy she had,
Who raised his forehead's calm her grief to quell.

Like one who by the troubled orbs makes guess
Of where an unseen planet shines afar,
By her emotion I could trace a star
Hid in the secret heaven.   Her pale distress
Bore record of a love no cloud could dim—
A sweet betrothal kiss—a burning vow—
A trembling marriage blissful to the brim—
A sheltering arm—a calm advising brow—
A death, a burial, and a loneliness.

What was the lost one like? The boy, I ween,
Reveal'd the features of his countenance
To me as to the mother's mindful glance.
Even as a painter's practised eye may glean
Looks of the dead from living semblances,
To clothe the child with age I straight began,
Adding Time's mellowing touches by degrees,
Until my mind caught vision of the man—
The buried man whom I had never seen.

XX.—THE CROWN OF SONG.

In days when monarchs fought and minstrels sang,
The harp was oft-times stronger than the sword:
It urged the patriot's cause, and wing'd the word
That flash'd a glory on the combat's clang:
Its music was a nation's sympathy,
Present applause, and Fame's enduring crown:
Prompter and prize of high-plumed chivalry,
War's shout, love's sigh, wound's balm, and death's renown—
How ring the names in Chevy-Chase that rang!

All records of brave deeds are poor and tame
To the full trumpet-notes by poets blown.
In many a stately tomb they rest unknown,
Lost to true hearts, and dead to perfect fame,
Whom no immortal of the Muses' court
In any deathless lay has sung aloud.
Fame, Fame! how is thy votary thy sport!—
To-day the idol of the shouting crowd—
To-morrow but the phantom of a name!

O England! when has mighty son of thine
Been loved and mourn'd like thy dead WELLINGTON?
From field and council is our hero gone,
But who may weave his crown of song divine?
We vow in bronze his memory shall endure,
And lo! a kingdom's tears upon his pall!
Yet on Corunna's height immortal MOORE
In WOLFE's fine verse has nobler funeral;
And NELSON livelier lives in CAMPBELL's line.

XXI.—WAR.

ALMOST twice twenty years of sweet repose
Had bless'd our land—when, hark! a cry of war
Clang'd through the isles. Muscovy's towering CZAR,
Whetted for conquest of his Moslem foes,
Had smitten Europe with a tyrant's glaive!
The shock that palsied Almayne with alarms,
Drew answering echoes from the Western wave;
The martial blood of France flew fierce to arms,
And England's chivalry in transport rose!

In cot and hall were women's looks aghast,
And manly hearts unmann'd in love's embrace;
Blind hurried partings left their scalding trace
On cheeks soon to be dried against the blast
Which stream'd a hundred pennants to the skies.
From clamorous shores went forth our armëd host;
Piedmont waken'd at their battle-cries;
While on their side were murder'd Poland's ghost,
And Hungary's tears, and songs of triumphs past!

Anon the clouds of war in thunder broke,
Lighting with baleful flames the Baltic flood,
Drenching the fierce Crimean land with blood,
And murking Asia's plains with sulphurous smoke!
The storm boom'd on. At length, when all were tired
Of mutual slaughter's awful holocaust,
Came words of truce. A glad salute was fired;
Rock'd every steeple; flutter'd every mast;
And in a grateful calm the world awoke.

XXII.—AFTER THE FIGHT.

TIME'S shore, that glisten'd in the sweet light shed
Of peace new-dawning in the turban'd East,
Was strewn with dead. Who spread the vulture-feast
Himself was dead—great NICHOLAS was dead.
Dead were ST. ARNAUD, RAGLAN high of mind,
And bold CATHCART. Dead, dead to all but fame,
Were thousands butcher'd. Where the wounded pined,
England's brave daughter of the tuneful name,
Fair NIGHTINGALE, her nursing sisters led.

What loves and hopes were hush'd beneath the blooms
That grew beyond the stormy Euxine's flood!
What gain had Europe from her drench of blood?
What fruit to show, save one sad hill of tombs?
Our bronzed and bearded warriors from the fight
Made England stand up strong within her seas:—
But flash'd no prestige of a higher might
From those who fell on fiery Chersonese?
Or sprang but barren glory from their dooms?

Thanks be to GOD, who made us what we are!
He fixed our fate—to lapse in languid age,
Or suffer grandly on a tragic stage.
The scowl of tyranny in King or Czar,
Quails at the proud defiance of an eye
Illumin'd with a fire of martyrdom.
Man wrong'd feels most his immortality,
And holds life worthless to the general sum
Of freedoms nurtured with the blood of war.

XXIII.—CONSOLATION.

*W*EEP, lonely eyes! whose seeing is in vain.
Weep, widow'd eyes! that may as well be blind.
The ships that come, uncared of any wind,
Bring many a manly shout and martial strain;
The wharfs are throng'd;—but you are lonely still!
Yet were it well to soothe your wilder sobs—
To gather calm from CATHCART's sacred hill,
And wear the sovereign grief that hides its throbs,
With wet-press'd fingers on the lips of pain.

In fancy I have listen'd to your moans:
They who had thrill'd you with their meeting cheers
Rest far away, beyond your reach of tears!
What public gain for your great woe atones?
Yet towers our queenly England calm and fair:
Well knew her sons the fealty they should give;
Unlacing fond arms at the trumpet's blare,
They dared to die that liberty might live,
And built us ramparts of heroic bones!

Who knows that herds might browse on peaceful downs,
Or rustling Autumn spread her mellow crops
For the glad sickle, over straths and slopes,
By happy hamlets and laborious towns,
Save for the guarding of our heroes' deeds?
Still, 'neath her ribs of valour, England's heart
Beats to a tender tune when valour bleeds:
She takes the warrior's, then the widow's part,
And gilds with homely love her high renowns!

XXIV.—THE MAJORITY.

I HAVE been trying, half a rainy day,
To count how many of my friends are dead;
How many live life's mazy way to tread;
And which are most—the seal'd in senseless clay,
Or they to whom the bland winds minister.
The larger number have their sacred lodge
In marble darkness of the sepulchre,
Or blinding light beyond. Wherefore I judge
That on my journey I am past midway.

And so, like one whose bulk of kin have gone
To some far land, returning nevermore—
Who wistful looks unto that other shore
As to his ultimate goal, yet would postpone
His voyage thither, having fond hearts left
Awhile to bind him to his native strand—
I think of those gone first; yet, unbereft
Of many a seeking eye and clasping hand,
I linger here, though white hands wave me on.

Oft as our trusting darlings to the fold
Of the Eternal Shepherd are removed,
Our links are loosen'd with the world we loved.
The earth is thinly peopled to the old;—
Sad anniversaries this truth avouch:
Yet soothing are the ills that by degrees
Make the grave welcome as tired labour's couch;
The cautery is kind that kills disease;
With breath of sighs truth's mottoes are unroll'd.

XXV.—CHANGED SCENES.

WHERE first my life its prattling course began,
Offended Nature gather'd up her sweets;
Labour and commerce and invading streets,
The slow sure progress of the conqueror man,
Threw doom of exile on the trampled grass;
Blotting the sky the smoky banners curl'd
Of toil exulting; slopes where once might pass
The herd's lone life were throng'd; the sunny world
Of birds was crush'd; the waters darkling ran.

Yet even within the batter'd thoroughfare,
Flowers of the youthful heart to beauty spring,
And root themselves in stones; the bright-faced ring
Of children in the city's gaslight glare
Gives out a voice of mirth as unsubdued
As greets the awakening stars on village-green.
So from the seasons in their bounteous mood,
Though scarce a greening bough might cheer the scene,
My heart drew summer gladness unaware.

Now, only now, alas! a sorrow clouds
My lapsing days, to think that not a spot
Unchanged remains, by memory unforgot,
Where I at last might rest away from crowds.
I mark the old man of the hamlet's love
For his first play-ground and his final bed.
'Mong sights of change my heart can only move,
'Mong unfamiliar scenes my footsteps tread,
And alien seems my home of dust and shrouds.

XXVI.—ASPIRATION.

O for a garden-croft of wholesome mould,
Small for my culture, whither I might hie,
Ere the day-lily opes its darling eye,
And whence, at waking of the marigold,
Flush'd with the roseate dawn, to my first meal
I might return with zest my boyhood knew!
My heart is sick for Nature, for I feel
Fallen out of harmony with her flowers and dew,
And gurgling wells, and musics manifold.

Last night I read the whole that I have writ,
Trying to wean me from my poet's dream.
I have been blowing bubbles on the stream
Of fretted Castaly. Fancy and wit
Are dull'd and mudded at their finer fount.
Yet through a dreary waste of days o'erworn,
Sighing of frailest things to swell the amount,
How many souls, in light of music born,
Sing to themselves, for other joy unfit!

How many stretch vain wings while doom'd to plod
'Mong limëd themes that snare the soul to earth!
In bloomy Paradise had ADAM birth:
Say, does a memory of his first abode
Linger with man? Oft do I yearn to find
A calm retreat where Summer spreads her gains,
Where the hand's toil might ease the jaded mind,
And where as freely forth might flow my strains
As ploughman's whistle on a moorland road.

XXVII.—FAME.

IF I must mourn my Spring of being past,
My older life should boast fresh wealth of flowers—
Adornings of the sunnier Summer hours
Of manhood's ripeness—thoughts more thickly cast
In richer fields of memory to bloom,
And catch a glory from diviner skies.
Yet falls a shadow of the coming doom,
As of a gathering cloud on all I prize—
A sense of loosening leaves and threatening blast.

Great ALEXANDER conquer'd half the earth,
Yet died in youth; and mighty CÆSAR wept
To think that he had lived like years, nor leapt
Into the arms of Fame. To feel a dearth
Of fruitage in our lives and springtime gone,
Is bitter grief. To gardens, fields, and woods,
Springtime returns; but ah! life's vernal sun
Comes not again to melt the wintry moods
Of hearts unhappy for a second birth.

And where are they who wing'd my callow muse
With words that wore a light of prophecy,
When hope was strong to mould its own decree,
And shape immortal futures? Ah to lose
Such ministrants to effort! By my side
Their torches sicken'd. Now that these are out,
All fame were dark, for theirs had been the pride,
Save that one liveth still to list its shout,
Or for its silence coin some sweet excuse.

XXVIII.—UNWRITTEN FANCIES.

In my young Summers, comrade of my noons
Of truant ramblings to the distant fields,
Where the brown linnets had their leafy bields,
Was a fair boy, who, as swift liquid tunes
Gush'd to the air and made it beautiful,
Would pause and listen with delight unbreathed.
Fine lessons conn'd we in that ample school,
And, graduates of Nature, oft we wreathed
Sweet-vision'd laurels through the flowery Junes.

He had a heart as liberal to give
As Autumn that unask'd by any wind
Drops richest fruit. His natural bent of mind
Was towards bright virtue, as the sensitive
Spirit of growth in trees is towards the light.
Beauty incarnating immortal love
He worshipp'd. In his creed the stars of night
Were GOD's own lamps, hung in the void above
To calm the shuddering fears of all who live.

In mountain solitudes he sang his fill,
But to the world was dumb as the shy stream
That o'er the populous plain pursues its dream,
And leaves its music on the lonely hill.
O world of wealth and waste—of loved and spurn'd!
How many fancies are as fleeting breaths,
Or last year's leaves, or lovely eyes that burn'd
In skulls that now are dust! Yet o'er such deaths
Awakes the myriad life that pulses still.

XXIX.—Too Much We Marvel.

*T*oo much we marvel at the things of old.
Too much we deem that Grecian love is dead;
That Roman matrons are no longer bred;
That modern women's wiles are tame and cold,
Compared with those that made the gorgeous East
A lap where valour slept and lost a crown.
Too much we fancy life a vulgar feast;
That love's romance lives but in old renown,
And in the passionate tales by poets told.

Never a glow of rapture would arise,
Never a tear of sorrow would descend,
O'er stories always read unto the end,
But that they stir some hidden fount that lies
In the universal bosom. If not kin
To the immortals of the vanish'd ages,
How do we take their joys and sorrows in,
Live o'er their loves in bright historic pages,
And bridge the centuries to blend our sighs?

Long have I learn'd of common life to prove
That in secluded nooks, where no storm comes—
In the recesses of well-order'd homes,
With no perturbëd surface seen above,
Passion survives, and burns, and yearns for wings:
That to our sober world there still are given
Enraptured SAPPHOS striking golden strings,
Distress'd LUCRETIAS going pure to heaven,
And CLEOPATRAS making sovereign love.

XXX.—SUNSHINE AND STORM.

'O JULIA! if a love no death can sever,
But stretching wings of hope beyond the grave,
Content thy wish, Fate's self shall be thy slave:
Small means well spent will prove the bounteous Giver,
While endless wealth will sparkle in our books,
And in the rapture of my JULIA's eyes.'
Content and pride were in the maiden's looks;
Her clasps and kisses made divine replies;
And HENRY felt she was his own forever.

Thrice came the swallow. A sweet evening's shade
Fell on the pair, all homely by themselves;
But HENRY, book in hand, was with the elves
On sheeny meadows where the moonlight stray'd.
At length, with sullen anger in her eye,
Kindled at neighbouring grandeurs, JULIA spake,
Like one who made a wrong of poverty!
The dreamer stared as from a dream awake,
And saw his fairy vision slowly fade.

Content was fled. Two reckless summers more,
O'er yielding carpets JULIA swept her halls,
'Mid marquetry, and ormolu, and walls
Whose mirrors made her proud! HENRY, heart-sore,
From costly goblets other comforts drain'd:
KEATS, MILTON, SHAKESPEARE'S self no more could charm,
Nor the new friends whose hollow laughters pain'd!
What next? A baffled hope—a fierce alarm—
Dishevell'd grief—and frenzy at the door!

XXXI.—A BRIGHTER CLIME.

'LANDED at last—the climate is divine—
I suffer little—I am strong and well.'
So wrote a noble youth in pain to quell
The fears that he had traced in every line
Of the loved faces he had left at home.
' The wind was fair that blandly wafted me
To these bright shores where not an angry foam,
Unless in storms I've seen not, frets the sea.
Here will I find the health for which I pine.'

Again he wrote—' I every day improve.
Oh what a fair and heavenly land is this!
It is a garden steep'd in Summer bliss;
The orange hangs its lamps in every grove;
The grapes are luscious in the curling vines;
The peaches ripen in the open sun.
That I may soon return I have good signs,
And count my weeks of absence one by one.
To ROSA kisses, and to all my love.'

In the next packet the dear hand was miss'd.
A stranger told how life had vanish'd fast,
Yet cheer'd with hope's faint smiles unto the last!
Even when a finger-ring his poor thin wrist
Had almost clasp'd, of healthful flesh bereft,
His talk was all of home! 'Neath simple grass,
Like England's own, he sleeps. Naught, naught is left
For weeping ROSA but a dream that was—
And sundry letters often read and kiss'd.

XXXII.—SEVERED.

IN zones of cedar'd hills and sultry seas,
The dusky nations dream'd among the vines;
But where the winds made fierce the stalwart pines,
Labour and genius spurn'd the couch of ease,
Drill'd the rich ore, and skimm'd the fields of light.
To broaden all the circles of the known
Men went like marshall'd seraphs to the fight—
Swam in the golden clouds that gird God's throne,
And forged for magic doors enchanted keys!

The stars they measured and the planets weigh'd!
From hieroglyphs of stone gray scrolls unfurl'd
Rich with the wonders of the primal world!
They the strong vapour and swift lightning made
Drudges for ease and profit! Not a shore,
Sweet bay, or sea-scarr'd promontory caught
Unmark'd the echo of the wild waves' roar,
Save where old Winter his proud fortress wrought
Of icy solitude and dreary shade!

Thither in vain all eyes might anxious bend
Through gray-cold years. Yet fancy shaped the gloom:
'Twas now a growing ship, and now a tomb
Of homeless snow without a human friend.
The loved were there, and had been absent long.
Help went when hope was dead;—but why persist?
For lo! a sever'd twain are all my song—
The fearless FRANKLIN fading into mist,
And one brave heart unwidow'd to the end!

XXXIII.—FROM MY WINDOW.

ALL day the snow had fallen in a white
And blinding whirl. But that the flakes were fair
As tears of angels, the bewilder'd air
Had been a chaos of dull spotted night.
The roofs, the window-ledges, and the rails
Were furr'd with cold. A tree, long obsolete
Even to the wooing of sweet Summer gales,
Stood like fix'd coral. Through the muffled street
Stole clotted wheels, and many a shivering wight.

Towards eve, the clouds had wholly shaken down
Their wintry fleece. Above the pale roofs gloom'd
A leaden sky, with all its stars entomb'd;
The frost fell bitter on the sheeted town.
At intervals a toiling horse went past
Puffing out fog. Back to my parlour grate
All warmth was scared. Homeward hurrying fast,
Went many hungry souls, with slippery gait,
And blue pinch'd faces pucker'd to a frown.

The long thick night was stifling in its arms
The shrinking day. Ah me! the houseless poor!
Ah straying sheep upon a lonely moor!
Ah weary travellers, ambush'd with alarms
Amid the whelming drifts! My heart was moved
Towards all around to act a neighbour's part:
Had any knock'd, how fain would I have proved
How Winter breeds a warmth about the heart,
Even as the mantling snow earth's bosom warms.

XXXIV.—HELPLESS.

MIDNIGHT! A female shriek, piercing and strong,
Wrestles with curses in the public street.
None pity—none obey. Once to his feet
Had leapt a champion to avenge the wrong
At woman's voice as at a trumpet's call.
The chivalry is dead in modern schools;
And that mad scream is lonely—heard by all—
As bittern's cry among the sedgy pools:
Distress is helpless in the Christian throng.

'Some poor lost wretch!—why stir? A sisterhood
Of sin and suffering has been her choice;
She reaps what she has sow'd—why heed her voice?
Such cries are common—they are understood.'
And with such solace to its sleep again
Sinks the soothed head. Yet she who shrieks and cowers
In murderous fear, perchance remembers when
She blush'd an Amaryllis in the bowers
Of rustic love, and life was pure and good.

Fell she or was she dragg'd? The shame and tears
Are hers; but whose the guilt? O age of gold!
How may some weeping memory have told
The household ana of her childish years!
How at her whispers may have leapt the blood,
Though now a city to her cries is mute!
Yet, at the anguish of her alter'd mood,
And at the maniac terror of her suit,
Somewhere some breast may shake with deeper fears.

XXXV.—RICH ONLY.

*T*HIS note came to me in a free glad hand,
Unblotted by a tear:—'Our millionaire
Died yesternight. I pray you, sir, prepare
A tribute to his worth. You understand
How best to word it.' Flush'd with honest shame,
I tore the insulting paper fiercely through,
And gave its hundred atoms to the flame.
Then thus I mused:—'Let the paid chisel hew
Ill-fitting phrases at an heir's command!

'The moveless marble will hold fast the lies
To one untrusted spot; and these the moss
In time will cover, even as earth the dross
Soon to be placed with tawdry obsequies
Where never Grief will hang her asphodel.
No ink of mine shall be made substitute
For the pure drops from Sorrow's sacred well.
Ah me! the loudest epitaphs how mute
To silent grassy mounds and weeping eyes!'

His death was buzz'd on 'Change. Some said, 'Alas!
How vain his wealth!' Others, 'His hugest heap
Could bribe not the Destroyer!' Quiet his sleep,
Now that a simple shroud is all he has.
I breathe no censure: what was due he paid—
What owing he exacted; he was just.
But not for him will I a chaplet braid,
Or to the spot where rests his unloved dust
Mislead one pilgrim. Let the poor man pass!

XXXVI.—WHOM HAVE I KNOWN?

WHOM have I known that I remember best?
Whom do I feel that I most truly loved?
Who fix'd his image never to be moved
From the clasp'd cabinet of my brain and breast?
Was it not he of wise and chaste desire—
Of brightest thought, yet sweetest modesty;
With tongue of eloquence and eye of fire;
Yet unaware of how he stood so high,
From never looking down on any guest?

Was it not he who, as a gracious knight
Curbs his steed proudly, rein'd his temper in;
Whose simple presence was rebuke to sin;
Whose manly charity was death to spite;
Who look'd on mortal foibles with a glance
Of tenderness; who knew to list as well
As to discourse with kingly utterance;
Who scorn'd to wound where if a harsh word fell
The wound were deadly as the adder's bite?

Lays of Middle Age.

To greatest minds the least is ever known
Of their own greatness. Theirs the towering thought
That dwarfs each noble deed themselves have wrought.
Likest to GOD, and nearest to His throne,
Are they who under blatant calumnies
Keep mute the tongue can fulmine to the skies
For others' right; whom simple pleasures please;
And who, o'er heights of toil and sacrifice,
Find their chief meed in thoughts of duty done.

XXXVII.—HEART-ACHE.

*W*HAT simple fools the tender passion makes
Of many a goodly youth! Friend CHARLES, I know
The coil that chafes thee;—I have guess'd thy woe.
Thou lov'st where love the fever'd motion takes
Of torturing doubt. The proud LISETTE has charms
As sparkling as AURORA'S pearly gleams:
Oh that her cincture were thy seeking arms!
Yet when thou fain would'st clasp her in thy dreams,
She is gone like Summer mist when morn awakes.

When thou would'st spurn her as a maid forsworn,
She calms thy jealous frenzy with a smile:
When thou would'st hang thy faith upon her wile,
Her looks are cold, and thou art quite forlorn.
Poor page! that bendest to her beckoning brow
When she would teach the world her beauty's state,
Her brooch or bracelet is as prized as thou!
She is a tyrant whom thy pride should hate:
She is a mocker whom thy truth should scorn.

Of thy own worth thy sense must be as slight
As of its precious freight the carrier-dove:
Why wreck the treasure of so great a love
On one who draweth from thy pain delight?
Leave her alone a mark for any blast.
Win a true heart, where comes nor storm nor cold:
So shall thy life, its perilous trial past,
Be as a billow by the headlands roll'd
To silvery ripples in the shelter'd bight.

XXXVIII.—EPITHALAMIUM.

SHE is thine at last—thy own adoring wife!
Thank the dear GOD for so divine a boon.
Heaven opes its beauty on thy honeymoon:
Thou see'st the light that when thy mortal strife
Is ended may be thine for evermore.
So full of happiness, thy bosom now
Can hold no pain: thou wert asleep before,
With dreams of anguish working on thy brow:
Thou now hast waken'd to a finer life.

Long hast thou look'd into thy EMMA's eyes,
And gather'd calm to make thy spirit strong:
Nor sneer of worldly pride, nor word of wrong,
Can move thee more to secret pangs and sighs,
For thou art shelter'd in the whitest arms
That ever trembled at a great heart's beating.
Already thou'rt in heaven -above all harms—
Above all envious darts, as vain and fleeting
As arrows aim'd at birds that sail the skies.

Thine own! thine own!—the heart is all surrender
That at thy first coy meeting throbb'd with fear.
Life's ills are otherwhere; its bliss is here—
Here in a love as exquisite and tender
As ever ripen'd to unrivall'd flower.
Should rapture soar upon a fleeting wing,
Thine be the deeper joy of calmer hour—
A balm for every ache that age may bring,
And for the gloom of death a dream of splendour.

XXXIX.—IN THE STREET.

A HERD of beeves chokes up the angry street,
Goaded by cruel hands; while, following near,
Some dingy sheep press on in huddling fear—
For tranquil pastures making piteous bleat.
Hemm'd in by snarling dogs, helpless, at bay,
'Mid hurrying crowds, and no green peep of home,
All stagger feebly past. Ah! happy they
If haunted by no vision of the doom
To which they go with blind reluctant feet!

Sad sight, alas! If righteous, who can tell?
Feeling is weak: GOD may have sent man food
In living shape, with finely pulsing blood,
And eyes of dumb appeal. Here, where I dwell,
The hunted mouse is murder'd in my sight.
Though arm'd for protests of defensive strife,
Small for concealment, or alert for flight,
On earth—in sea—in air, life preys on life:
In the red shambles all perhaps is well.

Yet from the ensanguined histories of time
Prate we content of Heaven's obscure decrees,
And take GOD's sanction for man's madnesses?
Feel we not rather the strong hate of crime
As our true monitor? So I, recluse
But sad and watchful as these poor brutes pass,
Even when I judge their flesh for human use,
Am fain to wish them happy on the grass,
And me their shepherd making grateful rhyme.

XL.—THE REVOLT.

Lo! where the Ganges winds through sultry plains,
The awful banner of revolt unfurl'd!
God! will the demon fires that fright the world
Ne'er smoulder out?   Must tears like thunder-rains
Still weep the lightning's ravage?   England's sons,
And more, her shuddering babes and frenzied daughters,
Have found such woe as the chaste daylight shuns:
Post follows post with tales of wrongs and slaughters,
Till vengeance riots in the Christian's veins.

Oh! dusky warriors of a fiery land,
If our brave slain were strangers to your tongue,
And could not move you with the accents wrung
From lips that quiver'd at a lost command;
If vain their pleading to your ignorant ears
As tortured billows the deaf rocks assailing;
Was there no eloquence in woman's tears,
Or in sick childhood's self-translated wailing,
That were you human you might understand?

In grief we look'd upon our loving ones,
And call'd them by their dearest household names:
How had we felt had these, 'mid shrieks and shames,
Found murder mercy under burning suns?
Britannia shudders and a moment weeps;
Then rising sudden, with her eyes aglow,
Hurls all her thunders from her giant steeps;
Yet, ere one bolt from home has struck the foe,
Far Delhi crumbles under English guns.

XLI.—VICTORY.

WE heard the wild roar of the cannonade
In broken dreams; and, 'mid the clearing smoke—
Oh never daylight on such horror broke!—
Saw mangled limbs of matron and of maid,
To insult dead, with flesh of innocents
By hell-kites torn. But lo! the hot air shook
With storm of steel, nor peace in British tents
Dwelt till for every gash a blow was struck,
And for each clotted tress a life had paid.

Honour to CAMPBELL and the dauntless brave!
Tears, tears for HAVELOCK, whose heroic brand,
From startled sheath sprang flaming to his hand,
And scatter'd lightnings to avenge and save!
Woe to the traitors! well they play'd their parts:
Theirs were the triumphs which a world abhors:
We gave them British arms, but British hearts
Beat in the bosoms of the conquerors
Who drove them howling to a felon grave.

O clotted tresses of the lost and loved!
O small gash'd hands that with the ringlets twined!
The fiery eyes of Vengeance' self are blind
With scalding tears. Yet, by fell suffering proved,
How England towers a giant to the world!
Weeping her loved ones vanquish'd, and the fate
Of HAVELOCK, NEILL, and NICHOLSON,—while hurl'd
Her vengeance on the foe, in pride of hate,
Her foot on India's neck, she stands unmoved.

XLII.—WHEN?

WHEN will it come?—the grand and gracious time
When the mild light that fills our Christian hearths—
Born of good books, and happy household mirths,
And poets' dreamings of the peaceful prime—
Will steal like morning through the city lanes
And tame the angers that make Virtue sad;
Thence spread a noontide glory o'er the plains
Where foes are met, till faces passion-mad
Relax and melt into a love sublime?

When will it come?—the reign of judgment cool,
When truth and right shall compass in one band
All isles and continents?—when every land
Shall glow with worship of the beautiful
In nature, virtue, charity, and GOD?—
When kindred, one in love through divers paths,
Shall have their semblances in States abroad—
And, as in households strange to hates and wraths,
The world's one code shall be the Golden Rule?

When will it come?—the age when to their den
Rapine, and lust, and murder shall be scared?
Still by our warriors must the sword be bared
Against the grim assaults of savage men?
Is the dream vain that, in some far-off year,
In its own saintly lustre panoplied,
Goodness shall walk the world without a fear?
When will it come,—the proudly prophesied?
Lord! Lord of Destiny! make answer, When?

XLIII.—THE RESUMPTION.

FULL many days I laid my Muse asleep,
Not through suspicion of a barren age,
For ever on my near world's shifting stage
Went by a pageant, with the phantom sweep
Of endless sorrow eased by eyes divine;
But those about me read no rhymëd books,
Nor hung heart-charm'd on any trancing line;
My thoughts took worldly colour from their looks,
And worldly gains were all I cared to reap.

Lays of Middle Age.

Proud Poesy drew back with face of shame
To see me temper'd to a servile yoke.
Yet, while I shared the social evening joke,
And loves and laughters to delight me came,
Was I not happy? Wherefore waste the years
A shy itinerant in the groves of song?
Even as a half-built house, when frost appears,
My rhyme stood still, and in the common throng
I moved unmindful of my nobler aim.

Yet once again! A lustrous eve it was
Of opening lights. For host, a friend I had,
Who, 'mid a round of faces fair and glad,
Shook off a learned load of forms and laws.
The talk was genial, letter'd, and o'erflush'd
With radiance caught from dreamy TENNYSON.
That night, beneath the stars, I felt all hush'd
At echo of a strain long-time begun,
And secret thrill of a remote applause.

XLIV.—WHERE ARE THE FRIENDS?

WHERE are the fearless friends who once were mine?
Can they be sleeping under earthy mounds
Who travell'd with me through the dim profounds
Of speculation upon things divine?—
Who, thorough Poesy's enchanted meads,
Were my companions many a blissful eve?—
With whom I pierced the veil of mystic creeds,
And, nigher GOD, first learn'd in joy to weave
The lay I offer at a dearer shrine?

Of the same waters drank we; and, in sooth,
So small our stature, and so lofty grew
The jewell'd herbage, we could nothing view
Beyond our teeming oasis of youth.
Embosom'd in a world of greenery,
Only when looking upward had we scope
To range at will. We saw an azure sea
Beacon'd with stars. Ah! blindly now I grope
O'er desert wastes for blessèd wells of truth.

O Heaven! how brief the span that lies before!
How have I profited this tract of time?
What have I done of deathless deed or rhyme
To be a joy of life for evermore?
If comes the seal at last of turf or stone,
Whence the wild wish round this death-fated clay,
With creeping age like Winter o'er me blown,
To feel the buds of a perennial May?
Shower down, ye stars! the ardent creeds of yore!

XLV. — THE INEVITABLE.

A GRIM and shadowy shape forever stands
In front of all humanity. He keeps
Watch for the sailor on the treacherous deeps:
His breath is heavy on the sun-parch'd lands.
The bribe of wealth, fair beauty's pleading tears,
Are vain to stay him; vain, too, is the appea
Of infant's innocence or age's fears.
There is no heart beneath his ribs to feel—
No yielding flesh upon his knotted hands.

Man soars into the wide eternities
Till, wilder'd in their awful solitudes,
He shrinks for soothing to the homely moods
Of womanly affection, and the wise
Calm faith of childhood, and the love display'd
In the familiar smile the season wears.
Yet soon the summons of the dreaded shade
Turns all his yearnings to intense despairs,
And all his beckoning dreams to ghastly lies.

What glowing heights of bliss were in the scope
Of aimful youth, if years would give him play!—
A knowledge wide as night and bright as day
Flickers like boreal flame about the cope
Of his soul's heaven. What wondrous orbs revolve
By him unmark'd! What lands around are spread
Unvisited! What truths he fain would solve
Are hid in tongues unlearn'd and books unread!—
Oh life, how short without the afterhope!

XLVI.—TOO EAGER.

THERE lived—I saw him oft—a studious man,
Who burrow'd secrets from the hearts of stones—
Dug from the stubborn rock dim wrecks of bones—
And of the world, ere ADAM's race began,
Bade them discourse in strangely living shapes;
Till, musing thus, in dreams unsoothed by sleep,
He saw, 'mid slimy wastes, fair isles and capes
Heaved up in pearly splendour from the deep,
And shining rills adown their sides that ran.

Alone with GOD he walk'd where the young past
Leapt into being. With far-prying look
He burn'd for light to cast on MOSES' book.
Creation grew around him vague and vast.
How days were ages, and great ages days,
He, MILLER, sang in unrhymed mystic strain,
Till, spying a beyond that mock'd his gaze,
He stagger'd onward with a wilder'd brain,
And burst life's gates to learn the truth at last.

In the thick eve is heard a whir of wings
Toward their sure nests. So may they make for home,
Who feel the aches of brain that madly come
Of baffled wanderings 'mong the shadowy things
Couch'd in far twilights of the infinite.
Time without end and distance without bound
Blind and bewilder our poor reach of sight.
GOD walks beside us upon common ground,
And to the near and known meek wisdom clings.

XLVII. SABBATH IN THE COUNTRY.

I LEAVE the church. It is a fair May morn.
The preacher's voice is frantic in my ears.
Earnest his aim to waken holy fears;—
Yet this bright hour I cannot choose but turn
From the majestic agony of words,
Lurid with curses of eternal woe,
To the cool purl of brooks, the chirm of birds,
The odorous meanings in the flowers that blow,
And endless blessings of GOD's sweet love born.

Lays of Middle Age.

The storm sweeps by; and lo! a zephyr fine
Dallies delighted with the flowery earth:
The hot volcano has a fierce brief birth,
And soon its ashes cool beneath the vine:
Pain is a little hour and health a life:
There is no anguish on the dead man's face:
Heaven sends a healing for all mortal strife:
The lightning flashes but a moment's space:
The cheerful stars through all the ages shine.

Yet what is Death? Why are we ever dull
In luminous face of such a universe?
Ah me! the shadow of the sable hearse
Falls like a cloud on hopes we yearn to cull
As bearing treasure of prophetic light.
Oh for a glimmer in our mortal gloom!
Oh for a voice of soothing in the night!
Oh for a hand with flowers of heavenly bloom
To make the grave divinely beautiful!

XLVIII.—THE GRAVE.

THE grave!—how wondrous is the eye of Faith,
That can contemplate where the loved one lies—
Track out through earth a pathway to the skies—
And clothe with angel wings the loathsome death!
Yet, if old miracles could vanquish doubt,
Not vainly would the acorn climb the air
A stately oak, nor even the flower bloom out,
Redeem'd from mould and worms, and strangely fair,
And crown'd with sweetness of its own sweet breath.

What are our miracles of human skill
But gleams divine reveal'd to mortal sense—
Rents in the veil that hides Omnipotence?
A vapour toils obedient to man's will:
The sun-limn'd picture shames the limner's art:
A word, a touch, and half the world is spann'd!
Each keeps its mystery in Nature's heart.
We only see what none may understand:
But that we see we might be dubious still.

Why stretch forth yearnings for the infinite,
Yet grope in darkness, stumbling by the way,
Calling forever for the perfect day,
Like BARTIMEUS for restorëd sight?
If CHRIST gives eyes our waking world to bless,
Why should life's torch the soothing heavens conceal?
Our hearts are bow'd with a sublime distress;
Yet Death how beauteous, if its night reveal
A moon'd and starr'd eternity of light!

XLIX.—A CONTRAST.

TWO friends are mine whose deeds all men approve;
Whose hearts are kindly as December hearths
When gladden'd with the immemorial mirths
Of dear old Christmas. Sights of suffering move
Both to quick tears. Their hands are prompt to give.
A word of falsehood or an act of wrong
Could come from neither. Knowing that to live
For others' good brings its own gain along,
Each reaps in blessing what he sows in love.

They have walk'd in charity a kindred way
Till near their end.   But in the soul of one
A trouble lurks, for he has ponder'd on
Life, Death, and hovering Fate, till light is gray,
And gray is dark, and night-fears come apace.
He feels a weariness, and would be clad
In the grave's peace.   Anon this wish gives place
To starward longings, whence he falls back sad,
Hugs the warm life he leaves, and fain would stay.

The other loves life well, but deems it vain.
Therefore he shapes a future in the skies,
And meekly dwells on its assured surprise
And dawn of victory over tears and pain,
With waiting friends and welcomes glorious.
When help is idle, he has words to aid.
He knows no doubt.   Serene he labours thus,—
Happy to live, yet not of death afraid.
Which dost thou envy of these aged twain?

L.—THE ECLIPSE.

BRIEF shadow of night's wing at noon of day—
Mantling with sickly hue the vales and hills,
Hushing the birds, saddening the low-voiced lls,
And tempting some few stars of anxious ray
To deem their hour of vigil is at hand!
In dingy chambers falls a fearful gloom;
The labourer pauses on his twilight land,
With puzzled fancies of a day of doom;
And crowds are staring in the open way.

What mask is that upon day's orbëd flame?
Is it indeed the moon that trails her night
Athwart day's face, as with a human spite
To obscure where rivalry she may not claim?
Ah! foolish to forsake her gentler throne
Where monthly she enjoy'd renewëd youth:
But lo! the shadow from the sun hath gone!
So passes error from a luminous truth—
So passes slander from a peerless name.

Great eye of day! this gloom our vision clears,
More than the mounting splendours of the dawn;
We see thee most when thou art most withdrawn,
Like GOD made visible through eclipse of tears!
Yet wert thou always veil'd—ah then the close!—
Spring wildly weeping her unfolded buds,
And Nature maddening to a grave of woes!
But there is order in the rolling clouds,
And wondrous order in the circling spheres.

LI.—POETIC MELANCHOLY.

LIKE one who pleases by his merry jest,
And urges laughter to the verge of pain,
Then, being call'd on, sings a melting strain
Of Doon or Yarrow, until every breast
O'erflows with pathos of his voice and looks,
So I, who own me of the joyous brood,
Weave doleful rhymes, attuned like summer brooks
To the soft sorrow of the poet's mood,
Thus seeming saddest when most truly blest.

Ever as human objects intervene,
Sunshine makes shadow. Round our shining day,
And round each far-off star's seraphic ray
Crowds the vast darkness. Round the oasis green
Burn the dry desert sands. Death bounds all life
Like sleep all waking. In the festal rout,
'Mid flaming lights and mad orchestral strife,
Come thoughts of silent floors, the candles out,
And ghostly midnight over all the scene.

Now when my days go by serenely bright,
I own it luxury to dip at times
Into the dream-world of my musëd rhymes.
My griefs are old, and none are mine to-night.
I could laugh breezily with any friend—
Roar over RABELAIS' or FALSTAFF'S wit:
But laughters loud come erelong to an end,
While by each dying couch pale Thought will sit,
With moistening eyes amid the quenching light.

LII.—UNDER THE WAVES.

THROUGH wilds of silent sea-grass, rock, and sand,
Where monsters swim and crawl—through slimy caves—
O'er peaks far sunk from any sound of waves—
Low trails the Electric Wire from strand to strand,
Or festoons chasms wide-yawning and profound.
Darkling it trails 'mong shells and floating forms—
Over the dismal faces of the drown'd—
Cold fathoms down below the reach of storms,
Or tides deep-heaving at the moon's command.

And on the mystic path of that fine line
Go wondrous messages. Far nations talk,
As near as arm-link'd lovers in their walk,
Through twice a thousand miles of awful brine!
Man's speech through ocean flits, like light express'd
Through the rent cloud. Knit be the hearts as now
The exulting shores of England and the West!
Proud Science wears a glory on her brow,
As newly-gifted with a power divine.

Marvel of modern days! Man's mastery
Is over Nature. By his sovereign skill
Her magic steeds are harness'd to his will:
Yet at his bidding while they course the sea,
In awed humility he needs must own
To claim the praise were impious and rash.
Great GOD! the miracle is Thine alone!
Thine the fleet lightnings through the depths that flash;
And their wild secret dwells alone with Thee!

LIII.—THE NEW-YEAR.

IT comes—another year! the voiceful tower
Proclaims its advent. I could look with tears
Upon the growing burden of the years,
But that a voice of childish joy has power
To scare the thoughtful shadows of the night.
Ah! well I mind me of the happy time
When I, too, hail'd each New-Year with delight—
With shouts that mingled with the midnight chime,
And drown'd with noise the pathos of the hour.

Time and soft song have made my sorrow sweet;
And of a hand I once might grasp and prize,
And of a face lit up with tender eyes,
Wherein the soul I loved had its clear seat,
A memory is left now calm and glad.
Solaced by song my secret tears are dry,
And all is beautiful where all was sad.
A channel'd grief my Muse has wander'd by,
And arch'd it o'er with flowers in tribute meet.

Mark how the eyes of little children fill
At every fancied wrong or petty loss:
Oh be it mine to bear each larger cross,
And at my manliest age have strongest will!
When life a daisied meadow round me lay,
Old people stood between me and the tomb:
Now that a rosy group hides life's decay
With garlands woven of the morning's bloom,
The world through lapsing years seems lovely still.

LIV.—WHEN I REFLECT.

WHEN I reflect that I was once a child,
Of cheek impatient as a mountain brook,
Prizing my ball more dearly than my book,
And spying beauty in the floweret wild
More than in any bloom the garden wears,
To me seems music in the playground's noise—
Hope for the truant who outruns his cares—
Study, not idleness, in wandering joys,
And summer days beside the brooks beguiled.

When I reflect what errors held the place
Of the new truths for which I battle now—
What grief has sat upon the sternest brow,
What tears have wash'd the most repulsive face—
How through all clouds of ill the virtues shine—
How 'mong base rivalries and mean pretence,
Beats in each breast home-feelings like to mine,
I grow more tolerant of difference—
More large in charity to all my race.

When I reflect how Mammon's paradise
The serpent mars—how death is in the gold
Which men forego the friendly grasp to hold—
How Fortune murders with her siren kiss—
Yielding the power that tempts to foul abuse
And the sweet founts of charity upsealing,
I prize the wealth that's given for simple use,
Not overmuch to choke the springs of feeling,
But for content enough.   Content is bliss!

LV.—MIDDLE AGE.

FAIR time of calm resolve—of sober thought!
Quiet half-way hostelry on life's long road,
In which to rest and readjust our load!
High table-land, to which we have been brought
By stumbling steps of ill-directed toil!
Season when not to achieve is to despair!
Last field for us of a full fruitful soil!
Only springtide our freighted aims to bear
Onward to all our yearning dreams have sought!

Lays of Middle Age.

How art thou changed! Once to our youthful eyes
Thin silvering locks and thought's imprinted lines,
Of sloping age gave weird and wintry signs;
But now these trophies ours, we recognise
Only a voice faint-rippling to its shore,
And a weak tottering step as marks of eld.
None are so far but some are on before:
Thus still at distance is the goal beheld,
And to improve the way is truly wise.

Farewell, ye blossom'd hedges! and the deep
Thick green of Summer on the matted bough!
The languid Autumn mellows round us now:
Yet fancy may its vernal beauties keep,
Like holly leaves for a December wreath.
To take this gift of life with trusting hands,
And star with heavenly hopes the night of death,
Is all that poor humanity demands
To lull its meaner fears in easy sleep.

Miscellaneous.

MISCELLANEOUS.

Waiting for the Ship.

*N*ow he stroll'd along the pebbles, now he saunter'd on the pier,
Now the summit of the nearest hill he clomb;
His looks were full of straining, through all weathers foul and clear,
For the ship that he was weary wishing home.

On the white wings of the dawn, far as human eye could reach,
Went his vision like a sea-gull's o'er the deep;
While the fishers' boats lay silent in the bay and on the beach,
And the houses and the mountains were asleep.

Mid the chat of boys and men, and the laugh from women's lips,
When the labours of the morning were begun,
On the far horizon's dreary edge his soul was with the ships,
As they caught a gleam of welcome from the sun.

Through the grey of eve he peer'd when the stars were in
    the sky—
They were watchers which the angels seem'd to send;
And he bless'd the faithful lighthouse, with its large and
    ruddy eye,
For it cheer'd him like the bright eye of a friend.

The gentle waves came lisping things of promise at his feet,
Then they ebb'd as if to vex him with delay;
The soothing winds against his face came blowing strong and
    sweet,
Then they blew as blowing all his hope away.

One day a wiseling argued how the ship might be delay'd—
' 'Twas odd,' quoth he, ' I thought so from the first;'
But a man of many voyages was standing by and said—
' It is best to be prepared against the worst.'

A keen-eyed old coastguardsman, with his telescope in hand,
And his cheeks in countless puckers 'gainst the rain,
Here shook his large and grizzled head, that all might under-
    stand
How he knew that hoping longer was in vain.

Then silent thought the stranger of his wife and children five,
As he slowly turn'd with trembling lip aside;
Yet with his heart to feed upon his hopes were kept alive,
So for months he watch'd and wander'd by the tide.

' Lo, what wretched man is that,' asked an idler at the coast,
' Who looks as if he something seem'd to lack ?'
Then answer made a villager—' His wife and babes are lost,
Yet he thinks that ere to-morrow they'll be back.'

Oh, a fresh hale man he flourish'd in the Springtime of the
   year,
But before the wintry rains began to drip—
No more he climb'd the headland, but sat sickly on the pier,
Saying sadly—' I am waiting for the ship.'

On a morn, of all the blackest, only whiten'd by the spray
Of the billows wild for shelter of the shore,
He came not in the dawning forth, he came not all the day;
And the morrow came—but never came he more.

Sorrow and Song.

*W*EEP not over poet's wrong,
  Mourn not his mischances:
Sorrow is the source of song,
  And of gentle fancies.

Rills o'er rocky beds are borne,
  Ere they gush in whiteness;
Pebbles are wave-chafed and worn,
  Ere they show their brightness.

Fairest gleam the morning flowers
  When in tears they waken;
Earth is bathed in sweetest showers
  When the boughs are shaken.

Ceylon's glistening pearls are sought
  In its deepest waters;
From the darkest mines are brought
  Gems for beauty's daughters.

Through the rent and shiver'd rock
  Limpid water boundeth;

Miscellaneous.

Tis but when the chords are struck
   That their music soundeth.

Flowers by heedless footstep press'd,
   All their sweets surrender;
Gold must brook the fiery test,
   Ere it breaks in splendour.

When the twilight cold and damp
   Gloom and silence bringeth,
Then the glow-worm lights its lamp,
   And the bulbul singeth.

Stars come forth when Night her shroud
   Draws as daylight fainteth;
Brightest on the blackest cloud
   God his rainbow painteth.

Weep not, then, o'er poet's wrong,
   Mourn not his mischances,—
Sorrow is the source of song,
   And of gentle fancies.

THE TWIN SISTERS.

STAND both before me; for, when one is gone,
I scarce can tell which is the absent one;
To stray asunder you should aye be loth,
So much alike you are—so lovely both.

Together ye are peerless, but apart
Each may be match'd by each; to rule the heart
Keep, gentle cherubs! a conjoinëd sway;
Our love's divided when there's one away.

Oh wherefore both so lovely? wherefore came
Such beauty separate, and yet the same?
Was it too great for one alone to bear,
That each comes laden with an equal share?

It may be, Nature, anxious to excel,
Moulded one lovely face, and loved it well;
Then, hopeless to achieve a higher aim,
Sought but to form one more in all the same.

Or haply 'twas in kindness to the one,
That Nature would not trust her forth alone;
Lest she should mar her looks with vanity,
To think none other was so fair as she.

If you but hold a mirror up to each,
'Twill name its sister in its lisping speech;
And still, while equal loveliness is theirs,
May one see only what the other shares!

Beauty that only looks upon itself
Becomes unlovely; yet, thou little elf!
Not even thy sister should be praised by thee,
Lest the harsh world pronounce it vanity.

Talk not to others of her silken hair,
Lest they should say, ' Thou know'st thine own as fair.'
Nor laud the lustre of her light blue eye,
Lest thy own glance win back the flattery.

Ah me! I wonder if alike ye'll prove
When maiden blushes paint the dawn of love:
Then will sad lovers, puzzled which to choose,
Find solace in the thought, ' Can both refuse?'

Then will the promise which the one has named,
Be haply often from the other claim'd;
And the fond wish of secret whisperer
Be met with—' Oh, it was my sister, sir !'

Go, go your ways, and in your little breasts
Still bear the innocence your joy attests!
Go, wander forth 'neath childhood's sunny sky,
And gather flowers whose fragrance will not die!

THE SKY-LARK.

WHITHER away, proud bird? is not thy home
    On earth's low breast?
And when thou'rt wearied, whither wilt thou come
    To be at rest?
Whither away? the fields with summer bloom
    Are newly dress'd!

From the soft herbage thou hast brush'd in showers
    The glittering dew,
And upward sprung to greet the blue-eyed Hours
    Seen peeping through!
Has earth no spell to bind? have wilding flowers
    No power to woo?

Haply thou'st gazed through the long gloom of night
    On some fair star,
Yet dreaded to pursue a darkling flight
    Untried—afar,
And now ascend'st to track by the golden light
    Its silver car!

Haply to thee alone 'tis given to hear,
      When stars grow dim,
The matin song mellifluous and clear
      Of seraphim,
Till envious of their bliss thou drawest near
      To join their hymn!

Or knowing whence sweet inspiration's given,
      This morn, as wont,
Perchance with eager pinion thou hast striven
      On high to mount,
That thou might'st drink the sacred stream from Heaven,
      Fresh at its fount!

Rapt flutterer! who may tell thy keen delight—
      Thy poet's thrill?
Upward and upward in thy tuneful flight,
      Thou soar'st at will!
Perch'd on the highest point of heavenward sight,
      I see thee still!

Oh marvellous! that thou, a thing so small,
      The air should'st flood
With voice to hold the listening world in thrall!
      As from a cloud
Most tiny in the blue, thy sky-notes call
      In descants loud!

What ear such bright entrancing melody
    Could ever cloy?
The healthful air, high-heaved with ecstasy,
    Thy wings up-buoy!
Methinks the Morning has commission'd thee
    To speak its joy!

Now that the curtain of the mist is drawn,
    What wealth is ours!
A liquid silver glistens on the lawn,
    And on the flowers—
As if the stars had melted in the dawn
    And fallen in showers.

Glad Nature seems the freshness to partake
    Of Eden's birth;
The very murmur that the waters make,
    Has tones of mirth;
While thou, to hail the glorious day awake,
    Soar'st high o'er earth!

Minstrel supreme! bold laureate of the skies!
    'Tis thine to sing,
In numbers snatch'd from Heaven, till to mine eyes
    All heaven they bring!
Or, listening thus, do I to that height rise
    On Music's wing?

By the Sea-Side.

On thy fancy, gentle friend! come listen while I paint
A little sea-side village, with its houses old and quaint,
With a range of hills behind, and a rocky beach before,
And a mountain-circled sea lying flat from shore to shore,
    Like a molten metal floor.

The noon is faint with splendour; the sails are hanging slack;
The steamer, pass'd an hour ago, has left a foamy track;
The fisher's skiff is motionless at anchor in the bay;
The tall ship in the offing has been idling all the day
    Where yesternight it lay.

There is not breath enough to wake an infant wave from sleep;
A dreamy haze is on the hills and on the shimmering deep;
The rower slackens in his toil, and basks within his boat;
On the dry grass the student sprawls, too indolent to note
    The glory that's afloat.

Round my throne of rock and heather the fat bee reels and hums;
The liquid whistle of some bird from the near hillside comes;
All else is silence on the beach, and silence on the brine,
And tranquil bliss in many a heart, yet sudden grief in mine
    To mark a stranger pine.

He is young, with youth departed; moist death is on his cheek;
They have borne him out into the sun a little health to seek;—
An old man, and a mother, and a maid with yearning eyes;
They smile whene'er they talk to him; he smiles when he replies;
    Despair takes that disguise.

Long months of weary watching o'er a patient bed of pain—
The light held softly backward that might show all watching vain—
With footsteps hush'd, and awful fears unbreathed except in prayer,
And healing draughts that would not heal, and whisperings on the stair,
    Are imaged meekly there.

Oh picture sad to be so framed in the sunshine sent of GOD!
Alas! those sorrowing faces, and such loveliness abroad!
I look a little forward, and I spy a wider woe—
The heather wet and wither'd, and the waters moaning low,
    And a church-yard white with snow.

Yet seems it well, my thoughtful friend, to cheer that dying eye
With witness of the spousals of the glowing earth and sky,—
To wrap that frail immortal in the year's delicious prime,
And nurse him into dreamings of the bright celestial clime,
    Ere falls the wintry rime.

THE STARS.*

[*Written in Early Youth.*]

THE little stars we love have tender eyes,
And veil them when the sun is in the skies;
Like nestling infants that repose by day—
Their faces screen'd to keep the light away!

But now, serene companions of the night!
Steal from your coverts of concealing light!
No sovereign lord forbids your shy advance,
Or turns you pale before his fiery glance!

I know not if to you our spirits flee,
Or if you rule our earthly destiny;
But in your silent gazing from above
I read a language of divinest love.

To soothe the sick, to solace those who mourn,
In night's dull chamber your small tapers burn—
A light too mild man's needful rest to break,
And yet a light to cheer him if he wake.

Miscellaneous.

All may not sink to sleep with day's decline,
And lo, for these the stars in beauty shine!
Gleaming like lamps of comfort hopefully
For many a tortured heart and tear-drown'd eye!

The maid lovelorn, the stars were lit for her:
A gift, GOD gave them to the mariner:
The outcast poor—to them the stars were given,
To show, when earth is dark, there's light in Heaven!

IN THE NIGHT.*

SOMEBODY'S wretch, not mine! a drunken brawl!
   A maniac reeling past and wild for fight!
   A shriek of murder in the hollow night!
But not a window answers to the call:
The clamour dies: again 'tis silence all.

No comfort, none, in the great empty street!
   Yet out I lean, regardless of the chill,
   And strain red-sore and weary eyes until
All sounds go by, and I in vain entreat
The darkness for a step to make night sweet.

Did but one orb look down with watery face,
   Some sympathy might reach me from above:
   But the slow clouds awhile have ceased to move:
A heavy gloom lies thick in every place,
Nor moon nor any star in heaven I trace.

Would he but come methinks I could rejoice,
   And smile glad smiles in spite of deeds unblest.
   Ah me! that I should wish to break the rest
Of my poor babe for lack of other noise!
Her cry would be at least a living voice.

Yet, darling! sleep, while I shut out the cold,
   And make for thee and me a cheery fire:
   Unhappy offspring of a hapless sire!
But that my years are young I should be old,
Seeing what I have seen and kept untold.

The stilly night thy tranquil breathing hears:
   Soft is thy slumber. Once I slept as thou—
   Watch'd by a mother. Could she see me now!
Maybe she does amid her sinless peers,
And asks the angels for some human tears.

Could I but think, frail child! thy feet should tread
   The path that I in lonely hours have trod,
   Forsaken of the world, almost of GOD,
Even while thou smilest in thy cradle-bed,
Upon my knees I'd pray to kiss thee dead.

And yet such innocence as thine should make
   Mankind all gods to bring back Paradise:
   Thy beauty, too, that wears a mother's kiss,
Should from that tender consecration take
A charm to keep it sacred for her sake.

So be thou partner, not in my despairs,
   But only in the love that will not end.
     Even him who has been, alas! my less than friend,
Thee I will teach to plead for in thy prayers,
And praying with thee half forget my cares.

What pride remains for anger or rebuke?
   What fire of scorn to comfort or avenge?
     Oh should I spurn him now, would it be strange
If on his orphan'd image I should look
And feel a pang beyond my strength to brook?

Dear was the garden where I saw him first,
   My hero of the gentlest perjuries
     That ever dimm'd with tears a woman's eyes!
Dear were the scenes where my fond love was nurst,
And dear the words with which my life was curst.

But hark! a step, more welcome even than sleep—
   A step—not his—hope comes but to depart!
     That closing door has closed on this crush'd heart.
Lone little breather in the silence deep!
The world is dead.   I only wake and weep.

TO A COWSLIP.*

No tiny alien plant art thou,
   But one to England's Poet dear:
The very pearl I witness now
   He hung enchanted in thine ear.

'Mid mesh of matted grass and weed,
   O unchanged Cowslip that I see!
What time he stray'd through Stratford mead,
   He saw and pluck'd a prize in thee.

'Twas in this narrow saffron cell,
   Where bees might poke their clammy feet,
That for the dainty ARIEL
   He spied a dormitory sweet.

As erewhile to his peering soul,
   The pattern coyly burns within,
Cinque-spotted like the crimson mole
   Upon the breast of IMOGEN.

How strong the life in things that live
   By Beauty and the Bard approved!
This pearly urn, these rubies five,
   Proclaim the flower that SHAKESPEARE loved.

And O proud nursling of the Spring,
   Fresh-born by haunted grove and stream!
He sang of thee who best could sing,
   And lapp'd thee in his Moonlight Dream.

Now here, now there, at his command,
   The light-foot fairies come and go;
While faintly from the silvern strand
   The airy elfin trumpets blow.

Strange things of life about thee stir,
   A sense of wings is in the air:
To thee, her small tall pensioner,
   TITANIA brings her jewels rare.

Thy lips with honey-dew are fed,
   The glow-worm's eyes thy glades illume,
Ethereal banquets round thee spread
   Make endless sweet thy breath and bloom.

O wizard wonders thus unfurl'd!
   Ye take the grossness from the hour,
With glimpses of a spirit-world,
   Through glamour of this golden flower.

THE EMIGRANTS.

THE daylight was dying, the twilight was dreary,
    And eerie the face of the fast-falling night;
But, closing the shutters, we made ourselves cheery
    With gas-light and fire-light and eyes glancing bright.

When, hark! came a chorus of wailing and anguish!
    We ran to the door and look'd out through the dark,
Till, gazing, at length we began to distinguish
    The slow-moving masts of an ocean-bound bark.

Alas! 'twas the emigrants leaving the river,
    Their homes in the city, their haunts in the dell;
From kindred and friends they had parted for ever,
    But their voices still blended in cries of farewell.

We saw not the eyes that their last looks were taking;
    We heard but the shouts that were meant to be cheers,
But which told of the aching of hearts that were breaking,
    A past of delight and a future of tears.

And long as we listen'd, in lulls of the night-breeze,
   On our ears the sad shouting in faint music fell,
Till methought it seem'd lost in the roll of the white seas,
   And the rocks and the winds only echoed farewell.

More bright was our home-hearth, more bright and more cosy,
   As we shut out the night and its darkness once more;
But pale were the cheeks that, so radiant and rosy,
   Were flush'd with delight a few moments before.

So I told how the morning, all lovely and tender,
   Sweet dew on the hills, and soft light on the sea,
Would follow the exiles, and float with its splendour
   To gild the far land where their homes were to be.

In the eyes of my children were gladness and gleaming:
   Their little prayer utter'd, how calm was their sleep!
But I in my dreaming could hear the wind screaming,
   And fancy I heard hoarse replies from the deep.

And often, when slumber had cool'd my brow's fever,
   A dream-utter'd shriek of despair broke the spell;
'Twas the voice of the emigrants leaving the river,
   And startling the night with their cries of farewell.

SHAKESPEARE.*

[*Composed for the Tercentenary Celebration of the Poet's Birthday.*]

LIKE one who deftly makes the puppets move
    While hid behind a screen,
My SHAKESPEARE shows the wonders of his love
    But is himself unseen;
And so I sigh, amid his wizard skill,
For one true look of my belovëd WILL.

What was he when he woo'd, by Avon's side,
    The damsels of his shire?
How walk'd he through great London's living tide?
    How flash'd his eyes of fire
When impious Scorn struck poverty to tears?
Or pined his heart at human griefs and fears?

Oh say, came kings to do him homages?
    Knelt sages at his feet?
Ran shouting breaths before him like a breeze
    Through all the rippling street,
Till clashing casements, fill'd with swift delight,
Went with him in a surge of 'kerchiefs white?

Or did my SHAKESPEARE toil in obscure ways,
    The light untrumpeted
That now doth shine to all the world's amaze?
    And as he meekly thrid
His course among the crowd, did no eye note
The dawning glory round about him float?

What answer find I in his magic glass?
    O eyes with sorrow wet!
O faces shedding sunshine as you pass!
    O lovers blandly met!
O godlike men, the marvels of your race!
O maids and matrons of transcendent grace!

Voluptuous Egypt scorches with her glance,
    White Athens floats in dream,
Rome builds her pomp, Italia her romance,
    The helms of England gleam,
Wierd Scotia towers in mist, the leafy smile
Of Arden breaks, and now, a Haunted Isle!

Amazed, but bending low to SHAKESPEARE's world,
    I list the loves of birds,
The march of men with battle-flags unfurl'd,
    Music and maddening words,
And happy pastorals 'mong the streams and trees,
And giddy talks, and gray philosophies.

But where is he whose witchery creates
    The things I see and hear?
On FALSTAFF's wit his vivid fancy waits,
    He wears the crown of LEAR,
From HAMLET's lips his lofty accents fall—
Oh wherefore hides he howsoe'er I call?

Through all the studious night I make my quest
    Until my eyelids fill ;
I grope forlorn, yet feel him in my breast—
    My witching WILLY still !—
And fain to realise his heavenly looks,
I steal soft glances from his deathless books.

O ever-gladdening smile of ROSALIND !
    O DESDEMONA wreck'd
Like a frail bark in a perfidious wind !
    O IMOGEN flower-deck'd !
O guileless JULIET sweetly passioning !
O dear CORDELIA with thy gray-hair'd King !

In your chaste eyes, ye all immortal fair !
    I see my SHAKESPEARE's face ;
And like an angel's is the image there
    That I enraptured trace,
Till, gazing, I feel nearer to the skies,
Being of his race, with upward wondering eyes !

HOUSEHOLD WORDS.*

WHY should'st thou spurn thy sister's proffer'd kiss?
And yet it may be mere shamefacëdness,
I being by: how else could'st thou despise
    What some would gladly prize?

But Jack! for she is taller for her years
Than most tall girls, thou banterest her to tears,
And call'st her 'gawky,' with full many a name
    That sets her cheek in flame.

Never a kindly word escapes thy lips
To keep her young bright eyes from brief eclipse:
Even when her playful arms are round thee flung,
    What scorn is on thy tongue!

Now, merry trickster! thou dost greatly err,
When thus thou triest to make a mock of her,
Who ere a few short moons will wake a pride
    In thee thou scarce wilt hide.

Gawky forsooth! such is her beauty's dower,
That at her motion she will yet have power
To lay awe-struck adorers at her feet,
    With flatteries strange and sweet.

What other damsel dost thou thus miscry?
One do I know, the terror of whose eye,
Though less illumin'd with celestial gleam,
    Could hush thee into dream.

Yet still, thou soul of mischief! born to tease
Thy guileless sister, half ashamed to please,
Or call her 'Blanche dear,' save in mockery,
    Thyself thou dost belie.

Should any dare to assail her, well I know
Thy chivalrous rebuke would be a blow,
Were he a giant that made fierce thy breath,
    And his revenge were death.

Still more: despite thy rude and taunting speech,
Should she be ta'en where love were frail to reach,
Ah Jack! thy heart would doubtless for her sake
    Like a big rain-cloud break.

For, underlying all thy torturing jest,
Is that deep well of goodness in thy breast,
That makes thee everywhere a favourite
    For all thy gibing wit.

Then leave poor Blanche her gift of placid brow
And tranquil pulse: let her be glad as thou:
That happy thoughts of these her early days
    May be her joy always.

Let sweetest dreams of thee, in years to come,
Blend with her memories of childhood's home—
Its daisy-chains, its innocent delights,
    Its kisses and 'good nights.'

Trial and sorrow will too soon appear,
To stay the smile, nor spare the speaking tear:
Then vex her not, but rather with thy play
    Make glad her life's young day.

If age should lay its burden on thy head,
And thou should'st mourn a wife or infant dead,
Oh! not in vain to her wilt thou repair
    In thy forlorn despair.

Or should some hope o'erthrown thy spirit grieve,
Some foe affront thee or some friend deceive,
To whom wilt thou so turn to still thy fears,
    Or share thy blindest tears?

This, too, believe: if ever fortune frown—
Yea, even if sin or guilt should drag thee down,
She still a sister's instinct will assert,
And cling and cling to thee for what thou wert,
    Though all the world desert.

ANY MAN OF HIMSELF.*

ONLY a fragment of clay
Where my bones they may chance to lay!
Will nothing more be on the earth of me
When my spirit has pass'd away?

Some souls that I love will fret
With the pangs of a useless regret,
And I sorrow to wis that the lids I kiss
Will awhile be weary and wet.

But the weeping will not be long,
For happy are laughter and song,
And time as it flies will dry the eyes
Alike of the old and the young.

And the boys will grow up with the years,
And the maidens be blithe 'mong their peers,
And poets make moan sitting singing alone
Their ballads of passion and tears.

And the noons will be fierce in their heat,
And the twilights be dewy and sweet,
And the lamps of the night burn down with delight
Where lovers in transport meet.

And greetings will blend with farewells,
And roses with asphodels,
And steeples be stirr'd with the music heard
Of mourning or marriage bells.

And wonders will burst on the ken,
And thrill from the tongue and the pen,
And the buzz of the crowd be low or loud
With an endless trampling of men.

And the trumpets will blow from afar
To the startling of sunshine or star,
And the hush of the Word or the flash of the Sword
Be mighty for wisdom or war.

It was so in the days long sped,
In the years of the tears long shed,
And so will it hap when in earth's cold lap
They have laid my dreamless head.

Oh! then for the wind's no tone,
And the thunder to me unknown,
While the centuries pass as silent as grass,
And the lichen is gray on the stone!

Deep rest for the relics beneath!
But the life that goes out with the breath—
It will not be there! then whither, oh where?
Being dead no answer has Death.

Elegiac.

ELEGIAC.

First Grief.

They tell me, first and early love
   Outlives all after-dreams;
But the memory of a first great grief
   To me more lasting seems:
The grief that marks our dawning youth
   To memory ever clings,
And o'er the path of future years
   A lengthen'd shadow flings.

Oh, oft my mind recalls the hour,
   When to my father's home
Death came—an uninvited guest—
   From his dwelling in the tomb!
I had not seen his face before—
   I shudder'd at the sight;
And I shudder still to think upon
   The anguish of that night.

A youthful brow and ruddy cheek
    Became all cold and wan,
An eye grew dim in which the light
    Of radiant fancy shone.
Cold was the cheek, and cold the brow,
    The eye was fix'd and dim;
And one there mourn'd a brother dead,
    Who would have died for him.

I know not if 'twas Summer then,
    I know not if 'twas Spring;
But if the birds sang on the trees,
    I did not hear them sing!
If flowers came forth to deck the earth,
    Their bloom I did not see—
I look'd upon one wither'd flower,
    And none else bloom'd for me.

A sad and silent time it was
    Within that house of woe;
All eyes were dull and overcast,
    And every voice was low;—

Elegiac.

And from each cheek at intervals
   The blood appear'd to start,
As if recall'd in sudden haste,
   To aid the sinking heart.

Softly we trode, as if afraid
   To mar the sleeper's sleep,
And stole last looks of his pale face
   For memory to keep.
With him the agony was o'er;
   And now the pain was ours,
As thoughts of his sweet childhood rose
   Like odour from dead flowers.

And when at length he was borne afar
   From the world's weary strife,
How oft in thought did we again
   Live o'er his little life!—
His every look—his every word—
   His very voice's tone,
Came back to us like things whose worth
   Is only prized when gone.

The grief has pass'd with years away,
    And joy has been my lot;
But the one is oft remember'd,
    And the other soon forgot.
The gayest hours trip lightest by,
    And leave the faintest trace;
But the deep, deep track that sorrow wears
    No time can e'er efface.

HOME TRIAL.

I NEVER thought of him and Death, so far apart they seem'd—
The love that would have died to save of danger scarcely dream'd;
Too late the fear that prompted help—too late the yearning care;
Yet who that saw his lustrous face could doubt that Death would spare?

Oh, could my pangs have lighten'd his, or eased his failing breath,
I would have drain'd the bitter cup had every drop been death;
But though I drank his agony until my heart o'erflowed—
From off the little sufferer's breast I could not lift the load.

It weighed him down; I saw him sink away from life and me:
Grief waded in the gentlest eyes; my own could scarcely see:
He look'd so calm, he felt so cold—all hope, all life had fled—
A cry of pain would have been sweet, but pain itself was dead.

They took his form of innocence, and stretch'd it out alone;
Tears fell upon the pulseless clay, like rain-drops upon stone;
They closed his eyes of beauty, for their glory was o'ercast,
And sorrow drew its deepest shade from gladness that was
    past.

The sun was lazy in the heavens that day our darling died,
And longer wore away the night we miss'd him from our side;
All sleep was scared by weary sobs from one wild heart and
    mine—
The only sleep in all the house, my innocent! was thine.

I made mad inquest of the skies; I breathed an inward
    psalm:
The stars burn'd incense at GOD's feet—I grew more strong
    and calm:
I utter'd brave and soothing words as was my manhood's part,
Then hurried speechlessly away to hide the father's heart.

His coffin-crib a soft hand deck'd with flowers of sweetest scent;
To beauty and decay akin, their living breath they lent;
But never could they breath impart whence other breath had
    flown;—
Ah me! affection's helplessness, when Death has claim'd his
    own!

Elegiac.

Our child was now God's holy child, yet still he linger'd here:
Could we have always kept him thus, the pictured dust how dear!
But soon the grave its summons writ upon the black'ning lips,
And wheresoe'er I looked for light, I only saw eclipse.

There was no loveliness in flowers, in human eyes, or books;
Dear household faces flitted round with pain'd and ghastly looks;
A shadow muffled like a mist the splendours of the day,
And sorrow speaking to the night took all its stars away.

No more might fair hands fondly smooth the pillow for his head;
The joyless task was now all mine to lay him in his bed;
I laid him in his earth-cold bed, and buried with him there,
The hope that trembling on its knees expired 'mid broken prayer.

As in the round and beauteous bud the promise we may trace
Of the unfolded perfect flower, I used to read his face,
Till love grown rash in prophecy foretold him brave and strong—
A battler for the true and right, a trampler on the wrong.

Had I my life to live again I know how I would live,
And all the wisdom I had learn'd, to him I meant to give—
To bless his glowing boyhood with the ripeness of my age,
And train him up a better man, to tread a nobler stage:

To train him up a perfect man the crown of life to win,
With kingly chastity of thought to awe rebellious sin,—
With all the lights thrown forward of a bright unwasted youth—
A soul as pure as cloister'd love, and strong as castled truth.

His lot, how happy had it been, with age to guard and guide!
And yet he might have proved a sire—his dear one might have died:
If so, I need not canvass more the heavens why this should be—
Ah! better to be early dead, than live to weep like me!

Tears! tears! ye never can be his! The thought my own should dry;
Yet other thoughts and sadder thoughts still brood the fountains by:
Why was a treasure to me given, for Death so soon to take?
Oh, may the answer be a heart grown purer for his sake!

Elegiac.

Striving one day to be myself, of living things I thought,
And musing on my blessings left, a calm was in me wrought,
Till gliding to my infant's room, all noiselessly I stept,
And shudder'd as remembrance woke that there no more he slept.

The world is emptied of my child, yet crowded with his loss;
The silence and the vacancy my steps for ever cross;
With every sound of merriment my sorrow is at strife,
And happy children stare at me like pictures wanting life.

My eye grows greedy of distress;—what healthless looks I meet!
What tear-writ tales of anguish in the harsh unheeding street!
Yet while the wasting griefs I trace in other hearts that dwell,
The sympathy I fain would give my own heart sootheth well.

Again, to dwarf my woe I dream of war and shipwreck dire—
Of choking pit—of crashing train—of fierce o'ermastering fire;—
Alas! the thousand frantic ills which some are doom'd to prove!—
O God! how sweetly died my child 'midst ministries of love!

Elegiac.

So gently wail, ye pleasant winds! and weep, ye silver
    showers!
Thou shadow of the cypress-tree lie lightly on the flowers!
The Summer has its mildews, and the daylight has its clouds,
And some put on their marriage robes, while some are clad
    in shrouds.

Thus o'er the gleaming track of life the generations run—
Do they to clodded darkness pass, or to a brighter sun?
Does nothing spiritual live? can soul become a sod?
Is man on earth an orphan? is creation void of GOD?

Is the resplendent cope of night deserted, drear, and dead?
Does no great ear lean down to catch the prayers by good
    men said?
Is groan of murder'd patriot, or shout of martyr'd saint,
As idle as on savage shores the homeless ocean's plaint?

Above the lands that front the sky in the illumin'd East,
The stars hang low and large like lamps at some immortal
    feast,
And from those lands so near to Heaven have wondrous
    voices come
Of GOD's eternal Fatherhood and man's celestial Home.

Elegiac.

I marvel, then, dear child of mine! whom 'neath the grass I laid,
If wing'd and bright, a spirit now, though scarcely purer made,
Thou liv'st in His almighty care in mansions of the skies!
Oh say, wilt thou come down to me, or I to thee arise?

Great mysteries are round thee, child! unknown or dim to me,
But yet I cannot dread the death made beautiful by thee;
The path thy little feet have trod I may not fear to tread,
And so I follow—through the dark—as by an angel led!

FLO'S PHOTO.*

[Printed for the First Time.]

THOUGH my lids are fain to fill,
Here methinks I see her still,
    Ere her sorrow came.
Will her gay 'Good-morning' break?
Will she answer for my sake,
    If I name her name?

Ere the sun this picture took,
Long we tried to shape the look,
    And the hair arrange.
Oh this winsome pose at last!
Oh this sweetest mood made fast!
    Not again to change.

FLO was Summer breath to me,
Music, health, and ecstasy:
    Yet her brilliance paled,

Elegiac.

As she sometimes press'd my hand,
Making me to understand
    Something that she ail'd.

There was blight within the blood
Of her growing womanhood
    That to hide were vain.
Like a canker in the rose
When its leaf the loveliest shows,
    Was her conscious pain.

Bright her eyes were with the gleam
Of the Heaven she saw in dream;
    But that light divine
Soon would be forever seal'd,
All the glory unreveal'd
    That on earth was mine.

Wan the ripple on her cheek
As she heard the breezes speak
    Of the health they'd bring!
Languid on her lip the words
Prattled of the flowers and birds
    That would come with Spring.

Elegiac.

When the pulse is beating slow,
When the lamp is burning low,
 Who may comfort find?
Utter love gives no relief,
And the helplessness of grief
 Gazes and is blind.

How I struggled 'gainst the gloom,
'Gainst the darkening hour of doom,
 'Gainst my failing trust!
What to do when all was done?
Naught I cared for 'neath the sun,
 Save what now was dust.

Where was any light on earth?
Any warmth to cheer my hearth?
 Was I quite alone?
Oh the mouth that Death had kiss'd!
Oh the soft low breathing miss'd!
 Oh the touch like stone!

Was that marble stillness dumb?
Or did thrilling sermons come
 From the patient look?

Elegiac.

Sore the anguish of my sighs,
But the silken-lidded eyes
    Lay like a rebuke.

Not a throb to meet my palm
In the depth divinely calm
    Of her sure decease!
All her secrets now were kept,
Like eternity she slept
    In her dreamless peace.

Who could turn nor weep farewell,
When I laid her down to dwell
    With the silent years?
Every turf that happ'd her o'er
Through the seasons evermore
    Would be wet with tears.

Round me all creation whirl'd:
All was Winter in the world
    Wheresoe'er I trod.
Ah! what mortal beauty died,
When her soul became enskied
    'Mong the loved of GOD!

Elegiac.

As the lingering dews, alas!
Would be faithful to the grass
    On her grave that grew,
So would my lone thoughts repair
To my treasure buried there,
    With a tryst as true.

Casual pilgrims might be seen,
Near that little patch of green,
    Making idle stir.
Not for me their careless laughs,
All my thoughts were epitaphs
    Fill'd with only her.

Luminous the golden hope
In her young life's horoscope,
    For she found a friend
Ever where her smile might fall.
Such the spell she threw o'er all,
    But how soon to end!

Now in cold defeat she lies
With the vague immensities,
    Leaving my poor wail

Elegiac.

Like the moan a small wave makes
On a shoreless sea that breaks,
    And of like avail.

What is beauty's transient glance
In the rapture of the dance
    But a mocking show?
What the Springtime of the year
But the joy that brings the tear?
    How I miss thee, FLO!

Grief on grief the day has dimm'd,
Since its light those features limn'd
    Here and in my heart.
Truth with fancy is at strife,
Yet how keen the glow of life
    In this life of art!

Hast thou from thy bliss on high
Floated hither tenderly,
    With thy filial eyes?
With thy pale impassion'd grace,
And a glory in thy face
    As of gladdening skies?

Elegiac.

O thou soul in looks and lips,
Deathless through all death's eclipse!
    O my risen star!
Age may strike its wintry chime:
Thou art no more touch'd by time
    Than the angels are!

Seasons ten have crisp'd the leaves,
Bared the fields and bound the sheaves,
    Yet how fair that brow!
GOD so true a limner is,
That fresh-born of Paradise
    I behold thee now!

From the pitying spheres above,
Com'st thou with thy human love
    To relieve my fret?
Had all Heaven no rest for thee?
Wert thou thinking still of me?
    Art thou near me yet?

Is it thou I truly mark,
Shining in the gradual dark
    Of this hour serene?

Elegiac.

Oh for one bright Summer walk,
With the sunshine in our talk,
  And no grave between!

Oh to hear thy voice again!
Tremulous with hope as when
  Thou hadst but one grief—
In the yearning wish to live,
Having so much love to give,
  And the time so brief!

Hush, O hush! yet soothly still,
With the gray upon the hill,
  And Hesperus o'erhead,
I can take thee in my gaze,
Even as in the happy days
  Ere our pearls were shed.

Miracle of life renew'd!
Victress o'er vicissitude!
  Spirit disentomb'd!
Mortal, yet immortal grown,
Still be in this vision shown,
  By God's torch illum'd!

Evening's drowsy veil is drawn,
Tarry, darling! till the dawn
   Of the endless light!
Be the daughter of my dreams,
But ere dies the day-star's beams
   Give me, sweet, ' Good-night!'

STORM AND CALM.*

[Adapted from a Prose Story by the Author.]

WHAT time the pulses of my inner life
Were strangely tender, with the world at strife,
And sick for sorrow of a daughter dead,
I met the man I loved. His age-crown'd head
Came with a power to soothe me and sustain.
From off my breast I heaved the leaden pain,
For he, fine-mettled as the stanchest steel,
I had known in other trouble quick to feel
And strong to help, half woman and whole man.
Yet when to clasp his hand I bounding ran,

Elegiac.

He struck and stunn'd me with a languid stare!
Helpless I stood with only my despair,
Like some night wanderer who, having hail'd
A friendly light, beholds it suddenly paled,
Or clean blown out by fury of a blast.
Ah me! that such estrangement should o'ercast
The eyes that else with mine had melted been!
But all is now explain'd: the vital sheen
Of those dear eyes was sheathed alike to me
And all the world! their blindness made me see,
And I am happy in the knowledge won.
Our friendship old has all anew begun,
Though something sadden'd by a memory
That while I live I never can let die.

Yes, I am happy—happy as an eve
When clouds that threaten'd take a tranquil leave,
Awed by the infinite beauty of the night.
Through every chink of Heaven there breaks a light,
Subdued and fitted to my mortal eyes.
There is no speck of storm in all my skies.
Friendship is mine, and love that will not end,
But with the glory of the future blend,

Elegiac.

Till what is best of man grows part of GOD!
Rancours at home and enmities abroad
Have ceased to be.   My heart is well at ease,
Steep'd in that sweetness of the charities
That still can pity where it may not praise.
GOD keep my footsteps in the gracious ways
On which 'twill be a joy to look behind,
Untrack'd by any howlings in the wind
Of fierce remorses ever in pursuit!
Yes, I am happy—temper'd like a lute
With all its chords deliciously in tune.
Not Heaven itself has any dearer boon
Than a glad heart with its own self at peace.
My life runs mellowing as my years increase.
Yet over all there broods a memory
That while I live I never can let die.

The Winter nights to me are very dear.
All the home voices that I love to hear
Are round about me, and at distance keep
The ravenous owls that kill the doves of sleep.
Humanity grows beauteous to my eyes,
For I have learn'd at last to recognise
The cheering truth that friendship may be true.

Elegiac.

Well pleased my thoughts their sportive wills pursue,
And laughters follow where the wit is bright.
My friend who sees me not fills all my sight,
And I his hearing fill with mutual gain.
More are we one that for a time we twain
Found through divergent paths unhappiness.
Greater the joy again to coalesce,
In simple trust, after some treacherous thought
A partial madness in the brain has wrought.
By witchery of books around us cast
Immortal guests are summon'd from the past,
Such as no single age has ever claim'd—
Poets and sages whom we hear but named,
And feel ennobled to be of their blood!
Yet though uplifted to that higher mood,
With the great bliss is blent a memory
That while I live I never can let die.

A little while, and she the hopefullest
Of the year's daughters—leading all the rest—
The HEBE Spring will walk the emerald dews.
A flush of gladness will her smile diffuse
Over the earth, making it beautiful

Elegiac.

As a young face fresh bounding out of school
And caught with sudden carol of a bird !
A happier voice will in the streams be heard,
And endless flowers make vagrants of the bees ;
While daylight lingers till it almost sees
The night-sky trembling with its wealth of stars !
Old ruts of tearing cannon, and the scars
Of cleaving armies thundering as they pass,
Time smooths and heals with silence of the grass !
So shall I list the great sea's monotone,
And think of trials past, of terrors flown,
With a heal'd heart and pulse of perfect calm !
Yet when the air grows precious with the balm
Of myriad blooms, and health beats everywhere,
Regrets will rise for one who once was fair—
By robber winds removed from my embrace !
And so, with tears upon my placid face,
The brightest scene will wear a memory
That while I live I never can let die.

Two Odes.

VICTORIA.*

[*A Poem of the Queen's Jubilee*, 1887.

I.

SILENCE was round me, flame and streak of gold
Had shrunk and paled in the declining west,
The dim historic page no longer told
A tale of splendour to my drowsy quest,
When through my closing lids there flash'd a crowd
Of helms and luminous plumes and pageantries,
Passing in pomp with meteoric gleams,
    'Mid myriad shoutings loud!
The great ELIZABETH look'd grandly wise,
SHAKESPEARE stood dreaming his immortal dreams.

II.

At sudden dropping of my book I woke.
Fled was the vision of that manful age,
When England spurn'd her spiritual yoke,
And DRAKE and HOWARD voiced the nation's rage,
In concert with the thunder-blasts that blew,
Till shatter'd was the huge Armada's threat!
But lo, the living triumphs of to-day!
   The popular love more true!
A happier Queen on England's high throne set,
Unstain'd by any blood of Fotheringay!

III.

Oh for some giant bard of that great time
To sing the later glories we have seen,
The newer wonders that have made sublime
Thy reign, VICTORIA! Simple Mother-Queen,
Whose influence gilds the continents and isles
That shape our ampler world! all hearts are full
Of thee where duty prompts or valour bleeds!
   Content with comfort smiles,
Where men confess thy mild majestic rule,
Thy fifty honour'd years of blameless deeds.

IV.

Let bells proclaim thy golden Jubilee,
From spire and tower o'er all thy shining lands,
Conjoin'd, not sunder'd by the wide-arm'd sea!
In closer union, knit like triple strands,
Be England, Scotland, Ireland intertwined!
Bid bonfires blaze, and chorals heavenward rise,
For freedom, to the TUDOR Queen unknown,
    Within thy realm enshrined!
Unstable were the birthright that we prize,
Save for its bulwark in the constant Throne.

V.

Crowns for the deathless dead who made our past!
Yet knew they not our travel's iron sweep,
Nor heard they far-sent whispers through the blast,
Or through vague gulfs of the bewilder'd deep.
No counsel took they with the distant sun
To stamp swift pictures for dear memory.
High-soaring Science, conquering in its flight,
    With wizard-power new-won,
Launches the mandate—let these marvels be!—
Like GOD's own fiat when He made the light.

VI.

In the far Orient, in remoter Ind,
Thy faithful arms repell'd aggressions rude;
And now are heard low mutterings in the wind
Of nearer troubles of as dark a brood.
But more this day's full argument has force
Malignant sophistries to expose and foil
Than red arbitraments on burning plains;
    While steadfast in its course
Our country moves, content with honest toil,
Unruffled progress, and enduring gains.

VII.

Ring louder, jubilant bells! tall banners wave!
And poets' hearts be stirr'd to joyous song!
Half of thy woman's heart is in the grave,
But all of thee that's Queen is brave and strong!
With her broad franchises for citadels,
Britannia towers to every clime erect,
Arm'd with the force of immemorial years,
    In sovereign law that dwells,
Slow to restrain but powerful to protect!
Take our deep love made deeper by thy tears.

VIII.

Proud Queen and Empress! thee mine eyes beheld
A child in Kensington's familiar glades.
Now life's young morn is turn'd to pensive eld,
But day is sweeter for its twilight shades,
And for the silvern stars we scarce discern.
So when thy millions feel in thee their good,
Let no regretful thought thy fond eyes drown,
    But be thou soothed to learn
Thou shouldst not weep if prayers could ease thy mood,
Or love make light the burden of thy Crown.

IX.

Gold to be worthy must have some alloy,
Life to be noble must be mix'd with ills.
If thou shouldst sigh 'mid this tumultuous joy
For the gray silence of thy Northern hills,
None will dare blame. Yet tender as thou art,
Be strong to accept thy later term of care:
Fear not thy fresh half-century begun:
    Wear still the regnant heart!
Rightly to strive is not to know despair:
Let hope new-waken with each morning's sun!

X.

Why at this moment shouldst thou not be glad?
Behold thy fifty sceptred years complete!
Oft has the doom of Royalty been sad—
Exile, a prison, martyrdom, defeat!
But thou from whom is nothing to be fear'd—
But thou in whom are all things to be loved—
Art safe in thine applauded eminence!
      O vehemently cheer'd!
The hands which wave, were need or duty proved,
Would flash a storm of swords in thy defence!

XI.

Symbol of fix'd authority art thou,
Unquestion'd in thine office paramount!
To that high office—then to thee we bow,
Not making thee of any less account!
For, though above all noise of faction, Queen,
Such is thy dower of gracious womanhood,
That most we love thy home-ways to rehearse!
      So be as thou hast been!
We name thy name—VICTORIA Wise and Good,
For patriot bards to trumpet in their verse.

Two Odes.

XII.

'Tis prime of June: the red-lipp'd roses burn,
As when the nightingales their love-tales told:
While all the flowers that greet this month's return—
The woodbine and the dainty marigold,
With fragrant flush of midsummer delights—
In rainbow-tinted broideries appear,
Duly their seasonable tryst to keep,
    And join our festal rites,
What time the days are longest in the year,
And scarce comes any night to hint of sleep.

XIII.

Therefore for garlands let the roses bloom!
Dear Widow'd Lady, who hast ever drawn
Meek guidance from thy gentle ALBERT's tomb,
May thy great Jubilee mark the growing dawn
Of that sure peace which keeps our island shores
Ramparts of honour! Long on this side death,
May time to thee a mellower fruitage give
    To enrich thy people's stores!
We greet thee, Queen, with shouts of loyal breath,
With high resolves that shall this age outlive!

XIV.

And when the flowers of many seasons die,
And some new Jubilee has come to strew
The land with stars and flags and revels high,
May Princes give to thee the praise that's due,
And statesmen, to thy best traditions wed,
Guard well their gift of tranquil government!
While haply here and there some aged man
      Talks of the great ones dead,
And of his happy youth-time proudly spent
In the old glorious days Victorian!

Two Odes.

A MIDSUMMER DAY'S DREAM.*

[*Suggested by the Preparations for the Glasgow International Exhibition*, 1888.]

I.

*F*ROM bustling thoroughfares I museful stray
To a new world of faëry round me spread,
Where classic Kelvin winds its sombre way,
The busier waters of the Clyde to wed.
O glorious sunburst of a summer's day !

What domes are these in Eastern brilliance rear'd?
What Kremlin with its mosques and minarets
Has in gray Scotland like a dream appear'd?
And lo! what gala throng the scene besets!

II.

Here let me rest upon this tranquil seat,
And ask where now is that song-haunted grove,
Where youths and maids were wont well pleased to meet
For happy interviews of honey'd love?
Ah me! the old simplicities are gone;
The woodland choristers are scared or dumb;
But the same sun that then in glory shone
Flings down its gladness from the heavens above,
While jubilant harmony of trump and drum
Makes other music than the cooing dove.

III.

Green lawns, inlaid with pleasant beds of flowers,
Which way I walk from breadths of sunshine peep.
Cool shadows cower for shelter 'neath the trees,
And cling half-hid about their barky stems.
Gay fountains bid the clouds take back their showers,
And, ever breaking in their upward leap,
Spangle the air with jets and plumes of gems.
Joyous with rival flags—red, blue, and gold—

The Kelvin swims with mimic argosies;
And in their midst what sight the gazer greets—
A tall-prow'd gondola from the floating streets
Of the ocean-city of the Doges old!

IV.

O wide-spread scene of festal happiness!
From stately Gilmorehill grave learning looks,
And in the living world descries not less
True theme for study than an anchorite
Might reach through delving in deep mines of books.
But most I mark these temples of delight,
Of modern years new-started in the van.
Scarce wore ALADDIN's Palace hues more bright,
Nor even the pleasure-dome which KUBLA KHAN
Built in the goblin realm of Xanadu.
Was e'er such vision seen 'neath Northern skies?
Could sprite of wonderland unfold to view
A picture painted for enchanted eyes
To match that day-dream of ambitious man?

V.

Golconda treasures, cull'd from many a field,
Enrich these mansions of MINERVA's love.
O Goddess! wise to instruct, and strong to shield!
Watch o'er thy votaries who worthy prove,

And o'er the precious things that in the hour
Of their completed splendour proudly blend
With all the sunniest growths of Kelvingrove !
Throughout these ample corridors what dower
Of genius stands reveal'd in dazzling forms !
So let me stroll from forth the open sward,
Which the ripe Summer with its radiance warms,
To where my thoughtful steps instinctive bend,
Moved by the hope of an assured reward
In full fruitions of all art in flower.

VI.

I cross the precincts in bewilderment.
Are these the grandeurs of Alhambra's halls?
O laggard Muse ! does some divine intent
Speak from the canvas of these glowing walls?
Move where I may, what effort and resource !
What dreams of beauty in new shapes express'd !
O dizzying labyrinths of mechanic force,
Revolving as if never more to rest !
O metals wrought for loveliness or use !
O textiles rich as from the vats of Tyre !
O industries magnificent, profuse,
Whether from distant shore or native shire,

Two Odes.

Telling of commerce wide as walks the sun !
O utter feast, too big for appetite,
Ending, yet still anew to be begun
Through strong temptation of some fresh delight !
O affluence, majestic, manifold,
Resplendent as the golden Orient,
Enough to almost tempt the idyllic sigh
Which he who felt the curse of too much gold
Heaved for some sweet relief of poverty !
A weight of wonder on my spirit falls.
Has some enchantress these allurements lent ?
Do the high gods hold earthly festivals ?

VII.

And what of man's device do men most prize ?
Great city of my birth, my love, my pride !
'Twas thou that tamed the elastic vapour born
Of elements whose birth-place is the skies,
And sent it forth a giant in its strength—
The brilliant Titan of our shores of Clyde—
To do the drudgeries of a world o'erworn !
Not in these temples does it only shine,
A toy to move the wheels that never fail
To draw keen eyes to marvel and admire ;

But over leagues of ever-growing length
It drives the cars with vehement heart of fire,
Or bears huge ships athwart the obsequious brine,
Nor waits a wind to bulge the idle sail.

VIII.

Ah! could our homely ancestors return
To earth with unforgetting memories,
And read of history this latest page,
Set forth in symphonies attuned to please,
With what new ardour would their spirits burn
To feel the forceful Science of our age
Shaming all prophecies the past could show!
How has the wonder of her wizard skill
Tempted and train'd the evanescent light
To print enduring pictures at her will!
While not even ARIEL's self with viewless wings,
Weaved in the magic looms of PROSPERO,
Could match the electric messages she flings
O'er land and sea with infinite lightning flight,
Like fire-fledged arrows from ACESTES' bow!

IX.

Say not these bold achievements of the years
Have come of elfin spirits of the air.
From busy brains that knew to think and dare

Have they forth sprung with aims more strong than vows.
All hail, brave workers through the frets and fears,
The adverse blows and battles 'gainst despair,
That score their rhetoric on fine-thoughted brows,
And compass triumphs often blurr'd with tears !
Hail uncrown'd victors in pacific fields,
Who, with no bugle blown, or flag unfurl'd,
Or store of thunderous bolts such as JOVE wields,
But labouring thoughtfully in obscure bields,
Have made for man a more exultant world !

X.

Emerging I contrast what I have seen
With GOD's own handiwork in tree and sky.
But lo ! what harmony exists between
What man devises and what meets the eye
Where'er the miracles of being stir !
Nothing supreme can man achieve alone.
GOD gives the inspiration that succeeds
To unseal the cabinets of the infinite,
And make Great Nature meekly minister
To the infirmity of human needs.
Who further drives the frontiers of the known,
Dwarfing past victories of sword or pen,

Wields but GOD's mandate to unveil the Might
That dwells in stars and suns beyond his ken.

XI.

Replete with contraries is humankind.
We court the new, we dally with the old:
Our steps are forward, yet we look behind,
And own a pensive pleasure in the past.
While breaks a future flush'd with rosy gold,
We clutch at relics to oblivion cast.
Hence is that antique story freshly told
In stately structure—like ALCESTIS brought,
A startling vision from the buried mould.
Stout buttress of the Church in ages rude,
Our grandsires saw it crumble stone by stone.
Where famed ST. MUNGO flourish'd, there it stood
For low-breathed litanies and leisured thought
Ere our great Glasgow had begun to grow.
Let Molendinar's flood make heavy moan:
The place that knew it may no longer know.
But now with sudden years upon its head,
See where it towers to grace our modern Show—
A pictured fragment of the centuries dead! †

---

† Model of the old Bishop's Castle erected in the Exhibition Grounds. The original building stood near the Cathedral.

XII.

Soon fades the sunshine from the fairest scene:
Of raptures and regrets is life made up:
We drink our sparkling draughts of hippocrene,
Then drop a tear into the empty cup.
O towers and domes so strongly visible!
Is that arena of Olympic skill
Where men contend—as on a village green
They boast the stalwart arm, the steadfast will—
Naught but a phantasm of uncertain sheen,
An Arab camp—to dream-like melt away,
The frail Adonis garden of a day,
Nor leave a trace to tell that it has been?

XIII.

Life's panorama flits by sure degrees.
What time the year is lash'd with wintry rain,
And leaves are few and stricken on the trees,
Our Summer's Wonder may no more remain.
But though swift-lapp'd in Time's eternal night,
The glitter may be gone, but not the gain.
Shall we not know it by its trail of light
In heart or home where'er its lessons reach?
So may the vision that delights us pass

Ere yet its novel charms have ceased to teach,
As passes some Heaven-gifted soul that leaves
Its fire Promethean to make earth more bright.
A livelier green is waken'd in the grass
Where some full freshet has its influence spent.
From beauteous things, though brief, the soul receives
New sense of beauty as from fleeting flowers
That come but for a season's ornament
In sweet apparels of the dews and showers.

XIV.

Be hush'd my song! Low constellated lights,
Full many-hued and wondrous to behold,
Throw flaming lustres to far-startled heights,
Or spread white noons through lingering Kelvingrove.
The multitude applaud the unwonted sights,
Yet with reluctant feet slow homeward move.
The joy-fires fade, the timid stars grow bold,
And peep from out the blue like night-blown flowers.
Now the large Moon, beneath a cloudlet's fold,
As through her silent heaven she sails supreme,
Looks on this world with a benign amaze.

Two Odes.

She lays her blessing on calm Kelvin's stream :
She tips with beauty all the neighbouring towers.
Oh for ENDYMION's eyes to read her gaze !
Methinks she shares the fervour of my dream.

Printed by the Author's Firm,
"Citizen" Office, Glasgow.

www.ingramcontent.com/pod-product-compliance
Lightning Source LLC
Chambersburg PA
CBHW032153160426
43197CB00008B/891